> Rats!
> They fought the dogs and killed the cats,
> And bit the babies in the cradles,
> And ate the cheese out of the vats,
> And licked the soup from the cook's own ladles,
> Split open the kegs of salted spats,
> Made nests inside men's Sunday hats,
> And even spoiled the women's chats,
> By drowning their speaking
> With shrieking and squeaking
> In fifty different sharps and flats.
>
> —Robert Browning,
> "The Pied Piper of Hamelin," stanza 2

RAT RODS

Scotty Gosson

Rodding's Imperfect Stepchildren

CarTech®

CarTech®, Inc.
6118 Main Street
North Branch, MN 55056
Phone: 651-277-1200 or 800-551-4754
Fax: 651-277-1203
www.cartechbooks.com

© 2012 by Scotty Gosson

All rights reserved. No part of this publication may be reproduced or utilized in any form or by any means, electronic or mechanical, including photocopying, recording, or by any information storage and retrieval system, without prior permission from the Publisher. All text, photographs, and artwork are the property of the Author unless otherwise noted or credited.

The information in this work is true and complete to the best of our knowledge. However, all information is presented without any guarantee on the part of the Author or Publisher, who also disclaim any liability incurred in connection with the use of the information and any implied warranties of merchantability or fitness for a particular purpose. Readers are responsible for taking suitable and appropriate safety measures when performing any of the operations or activities described in this work.

All trademarks, trade names, model names and numbers, and other product designations referred to herein are the property of their respective owners and are used solely for identification purposes. This work is a publication of CarTech, Inc., and has not been licensed, approved, sponsored, or endorsed by any other person or entity. The publisher is not associated with any product, service, or vendor mentioned in this book, and does not endorse the products or services of any vendor mentioned in this book.

Edit by Scott Parkhurst
Layout by Monica Seiberlich

ISBN 978-1-61325-332-8
Item No. CT486P

Library of Congress Cataloging-in-Publication Data

Gosson, Scotty.
 Rat rods : rodding's imperfect stepchildren / By Scotty Gosson.
   p. cm.
 ISBN 978-1-934709-21-4
 1. Hot rods. I. Title.

TL236.3.G67 2012
629.228'6–dc23
                              2011032183

Printed in USA

Cover Photo:
Chuck Motzko's Model A Pickup instantly turns the most idyllic setting into a crime scene. (Photo Courtesy Scott Parkhurst)

Title Page:
Troy Nichols' 1940 Ford pickup even has a demanding presence while parked. It goes pretty good, too. (Photo Courtesy Byron Kane)

Contents Page
Top:
Randy Ellis' Jeep, happily lost in the desert. (Photo Courtesy Christain Hazel)

Bottom:
Dennis Bradford's modified Dodge holds helpless passengers hostage on the wrong side of the car. (Photo Courtesy Collin Surbert)

Page 6:
Tyler Souter's Model A coupe is full-time cool, thanks to A/C and glass delete. (Photo Courtesy Rory Bright)

Page 7:
Andy Watley's Chevy coupe, making tracks to Point B. (Photo Courtesy Dave Taylor)

Page 8:
Dennis Bradford's modified Dodge evokes bulldog stance and attitude. (Photo Courtesy Collin Surbert)

Back Cover Photos
Top:
Dylan Patterson's Tudor represents the tin within. (Photo Courtesy Scott Parkhurst)

Bottom:
Troy Washer's 1957 Pontiac and Mike Bermudez's Ford truck say it in unison: "Yeah, you grabbed the right book!"

CONTENTS

ACKNOWLEDGMENTS ... 6

ABOUT THE AUTHOR ... 7

FOREWORD BY TIM BERNSAU ... 8

INTRODUCTION ... 9

Chapter 1: Rat Embryos— Egads! A Niche Tradition is Born ... 10

Chapter 2: The Resurgence of Unfinished Cars— Drinking Koolaid While Driving Over Cliffs ... 14

Chapter 3: The Trend Catches Fire— Respectable Rats? Going Mainstream at Full-Volume Swagger ... 70

Chapter 4: A New Breed of Extreme Rods— XXX Hardcore Bare Metal Photos! You must Be 18 to View this Chapter ... 92

Chapter 5: Shock Value with a Grin— Oh Yeah?! Get a Load of This ... 130

Chapter 6: Hightailing It into The Future— Fearless Explorers Discover Future Based on Past. Tonight, on Newswatch at 11:00 ... 144

EPILOGUE ... 158

ACKNOWLEDGMENTS

Saint Shellski—Patron Saint of deadbeat boyfriends.
Scott Parkhurst—Editor Emeritus.
Tim Bernsau—All Star Foreword.

For the first time, I had some photographers in the field. A snappy tip of the lens cap to: Richard Toonkel at Auto Photo in New Jersey; Joe Wongananda in Maryland. Scott "f8" Parkhurst contributed a number of photo features. These guys all know their stuff and saved me from Blank Page Syndrome. Thanks!

Richard Fleener from Legendary Collector Cars helped me sniff out some particularly elusive rats.

Mike Szuba from Jalopyrama also coaxed out some shy rats for me.

Mark Skipper (AKA "Royal Shifter") contributed some historical images from his bottomless photo warehouse.

My deepest gratitude goes to all the builders/owners who permitted me to gratuitously exploit their cars in this book. Some were friends, while many were strangers when we first crossed paths (some stranger than others). Some were discovered in online forums such as Rat Rods Rule and Kill Billet. A few came from the H.A.M.B., but begged me not to tell (you didn't hear that from me). All of them are gifted craftsmen and brave scouts, with a passion for kicking the creative spirit out of the shadows and into the next phase of rodding's time continuum. You guys are new era pioneers.

ABOUT THE AUTHOR

You don't know me—I'm nobody. But I know things. Things deemed valuable enough to print, apparently. I don't "get" that, but I'll take it. The truth is, I'm just a hitchhiker—lucky enough to cross paths with some amazing people and ride shotgun on their adventure until it becomes part of my own, then I relay the news to you and stumble on to the next one. This makes me very happy. I'm the Forrest Gump of hot rodding. I don't know how this happens, but I do know I'm the luckiest guy in town. That's what I know.

Here are a few other tidbits.. . . .

Born and raised in northern Oregon (born 1956). Learned to read and write via older brother Wayne's car magazines.

Dad was a welder and biker (our family car was a full-race 1948 Harley flathead with no fenders, open headers, suicide clutch, solo seat, and no brakes). We had other vehicles, but the bike was usually the only one standing after a couple weeks.

Got first car running (1953 Ford two-door wagon) at age 12. Left home at age 14 to street race full time (with SBC straight-axle '58 Anglia).

Started working in wrecking yards at 15. Wheel and track mechanic in Army at age 17. Professional musician (singer-songwriter). Parts fabricator at Bob Drake Reproductions. Began freelance chassis fabrication biz at Steve's Auto Restoration in 2001. Worked at many race car/rod/custom shops until the economy got me in 2009. Work part time as Tech Inspector and Announcer at local drag strip (Champion Raceway). Play original hot rod music at local venues as time allows.

Began freelancing for magazines in 2002, and have been published in *Drag Racing USA*, *Car Culture Deluxe*, *Car Craft*, *Rod & Custom*, *Hot Rod*, *Hot Rod Deluxe,* and *Goodguys Gazette*.

Built many street/strip cars for myself over the years and had too many adventures to remember.

Currently live in southern Oregon with long-time girlfriend, Shellski, and Sheila the Wonder Dog. Future plans are to finish my eternal Altered project and race it to death. Also hope to write a lot more books (and songs). But, I've already had way more than my share of fun, so I'm fine with whatever happens.

Foreword

RAT IS IN THE EYE OF THE BEHOLDER

A number of years ago, somebody (nobody knows who) coined a term for stripped down, hopped up traditional American iron—homebuilt and homely cars, rough but tough, built with more attention to performance than to style or creature comforts. The term used to describe them was reviled by many of the guys who built and drove those cars, but it caught on fast and never went away. The term is "hot rod."

An editorial in a 1947 issue of the SCTA *Racing News* insisted, "We're not hot rods" and discouraged the use of the ignoble term. A few months later, *Racing News* editor Wally Parks helped establish a new magazine actually called *Hot Rod*. A few years after that, Parks founded the National Hot Rod Association. Today, many enthusiasts insist on being called hot rodders and have directed their scorn toward a newer term. That term is "rat rod."

What is a rat rod, anyway? I get different answers from everybody I ask, but most of the answers run along the lines of, "I know one when I see one." A poorly built, rust devoured hulk with a 4-inch windshield, no top, no floor, no paint, and an overturned wire milk crate for a seat seems to fit most people's definition of a rat rod, but I've heard the term used to describe well-built, traditionally styled cars, too. One knowledgeable friend of mine applied the term to the Eastwood & Barakat '32 sedan—the homebuilt-in-a-hurry budget bomber from 1982, honored a few years ago as one of the "75 Most Significant '32 Fords of All Time." A prominent magazine used the phrase "rat rod proportions" when describing an immaculate, six-years-in-the-making Model A roadster pickup that was an America's Most Beautiful Roadster contender in 2009. Is there anything "rat" about either of these cars? The answer is no . . . or yes. It depends on whom you ask.

Some rodders hate the term. Tell a guy who worked hard to replicate the authentic look of a prewar dry lakes racer that he drives a rat rod and you might get a finger in your chest and an ear full of choice words to tell you, "We're not rat rods." Other rodders embrace the rat rod label, even promoting it with rodent themed graphics and accessories, not to mention mechanical and style modifications made in an effort to out-rat the next guy.

Like 'em or not, rat rods caught on fast and show no sign of disappearing—which raises some questions. If the goal is to look ratty, is there such a thing as a well-done rat rod? As the aftermarket embraces them, could we see a rat rod built entirely from aftermarket parts? Will a rat rod ever win America's Most Beautiful Roadster? We'll find out, I guess. For now, I'm going back to my original question: What is a rat rod, anyway? I'm looking forward to learning how Scotty Gosson answers that one.

—Tim Bernsau
Veteran magazine feature editor, most recently with *Rod & Custom* and *Street Rodder* magazines.

INTRODUCTION

Rat rods are a pie in the face of the status quo, which is crucial to evolution. If you don't believe me, just ask the Marx Brothers. Some see the rats as a call to anarchy. I think it's healthy to shake things up a bit, so this book celebrates the free-range thinking and broken-chain spirits of the rat rod builder/driver. Sorry, but rats are just too damn shifty to define or analyze—they refuse to be labeled and boxed up for mass consumption—a waste of cheese. My approach to the subject is more straight-on, as evidenced by these scribbled notes from an early meeting on this project: "Rat rods are the court jesters of hot rodding . . . They get no respect and ask for none . . . By begging not to be taken seriously, rat rods force low expectations and deliver handily . . . They are the lowest of the lowbrow—the most garage of bands." The primary aspect endearing rat rods to us is that they're home-built—cars don't get any more personal than that. Sorry, haters, but this is true grassroots hot rodding. Rats carry that tradition forward fast and loud with a swagger and a grin, but by God, they carry it.

That pretty much sums up my perception of them, anyway.

Rat rodders and their fans would be aghast to find they'd forked over their hard-earned book allowance for a dry dissertation of the phenomenon that provides the maximum yuk per buck ratio on wheels. Screw that. I'm just a fan, like you. For me, hanging with these guys was akin to joining Keith Richards for a weekend in Juarez. I stumbled across these characters and got to ride shotgun on their adventures of envisioning, building, and driving these machines. It was giddy manic fun, scary dangerous at times, usually insightful, and always a kick in the pants! I'm just grateful to have survived with my wallet and no STDs. More than anything, I'm humbled to have crossed paths with these prodigious spirits of hot rodding's deepest roots. Thanks for the reminders, guys—lest we take ourselves too seriously . . .

Rat rods make great first-time builder projects. Any budget is just right and there's no rulebook dictating which elements are correct or incorrect—the builder's imagination, intuition, and sense of humor are the only guidelines. Tastes and skills vary, just like anywhere else, but there's no right or wrong way to do this. Some people get so caught up in the creative freedom that they swear allegiance as rats-for-life, while others move on to other gearhead niches—typically, traditional rods and/or customs. And many in-progress traditional rods and customs get mislabeled as rats. That's just one more reason why I don't read labels. I see hot rodding as one big party, so I've thrown in some of these "accidental rats" as well.

Personally, I learned some ugly truths about myself upon initially balking at this assignment. I looked long and hard at my judgmental attitude toward the rats before realizing they were challenging my rigid preconceptions of order—mixing up build styles (like customs, beaters, show cars, lowriders, and racers) so loose and fast was just too chaotic for my bourgeois sensibilities to handle. While thinking back to how I'd developed such a black-and-white view of rodding (gack!), I remembered where I came from: I'd snuck into rodding through a rat hole myself!

My first exposure to this stuff was as a punk kid in small town America in the early 1960s. Some of the local farm kids would yank retired flatbed dually work trucks from their comas and cut them down to a stubby wheelbase, flip the front axle over the springs for some rake, and slide in a junkyard V-8 (or not), then cruise for laughs downtown. They usually kept the bodies au naturel, except for occasional hand-lettered slogans ("Beat Prineville!" or "Kegger Courtesy Shuttle"), just to drive the silliness home. These things were rolling parties, with as many revelers as possible jammed into the cab and stacked up on the miniscule flatbeds. They were a welcome relief from the tension created by the hordes of gnarly street racers (and the surly cops they attracted) that ruled our town's main drag. I fell hard for them and have been addicted ever since.

To this day, I have a soft spot in my head for anything crusty and whimsical. So it's no surprise that although I'd spend most of my life helping others build fast and beautiful cars, my own junk was sometimes fast, but never beautiful (at least not in the socially accepted sense). I'm comfy with that. I'll admit to some trepidation when beaters were received as fringe cars among the more mainstream rodding scene and suddenly, my "norm" was someone else's novelty. But after a few minutes, I got over it and just did my thing, without concern that it might be this week's trend.

So now you know where I'm coming from. Think you still want to continue with this read? Consider your choice carefully—you might not be ready for this. Take your time. When you're sufficiently braced for it, my take on rat rodding is waiting on the next page . . .

Chapter 1
RAT EMBRYOS —EGADS!

This made it official—there are no more rules! There was no holding back the rats once The Shifters' Marky Idzardi built The Purple People Eater. *And the best part is it actually runs and drives. In fact, it's made some early lift dragstrip passes in the 11.60s, while frying the tires through the lights at 105 mph. Marky says, "I sit really low in it, so I have pretty good vision, actually. Until it's really haulin', then everything's just a blur. But I'm used to that now." Many credit the Shifters' Anthony Casteneda with coining the "rat rod" moniker in 1994. These visionaries are still going flat out today, in southern California. (Photo Courtesy Marky Idzardi)*

A NICHE TRADITION IS BORN.

he hot rod world is big enough for everyone and these cars were accepted in the spirit they introduced themselves with. After all, it's all about having fun with cars, right?

When the first horseless carriage crashed, carnivores were most likely waiting to pick parts off it to fulfill some twisted vision of what could be. These events undoubtedly inspired someone to open the first wrecking yard. Soon after, the first rat rod probably tripped over its tail, taking its first wobbly baby steps before anyone thought to catch the event on film. The rats have been multiplying at a steady pace ever since.

The early rats were borne of diverse parentage. Mothered by necessity in rural America, homebuilt contraptions conjured from scraps were employed as cheap alternatives to expensive farm equipment, doing a lot more chores than entertaining. Of course, it was only a matter of time before Junior paraded Dad's doodlebug through town with a wink and a grin, receiving just as much attention as the rich kid's shiny new convertible—just a different kind of attention. But it worked, prying open doors that had previously been slammed shut in the faces of these outcasts.

Fathered by returning World War II vets intent on fixing their adrenaline jones, rats were there for the restart of hot rodding: Soup jobs were built as tributes (and sacrifices) to the Speed Gods; lead sleds were sculpted as artistic statements; and a big handful of funmobiles just showed up for the party, displaying enigmatic visual clues of their intentions, such as raccoon tails, whacky horns, and hand-lettered messages to the general public ("Kilroy was Here!").

Luckily, the hot rod world is big enough for everyone and these cars were accepted in the spirit they introduced themselves with. After all, it's all about having fun with cars, right? So the razzing began, with good-natured shouts of "jalopy," "beater," "clown car," "shot rod," "crap wagon," and more that I can't print here. The die was cast and a niche tradition born.

In that light, here's some graphic proof of the beaters that would come to be called rat rods.

John Shalestock terrorized Olney, Maryland, with this 2¾-inch sectioned street/strip Deuce in 1959. It later ran a dual-quad Corvette mill, when the Shalestock brothers competed in B/SR. A little rough around the edges, but plenty fast. Best part is brother Gerry still drives it today, unrestored. (Photo Courtesy Charles Shalestock)

Top: Carl Lembke shot his Deuce five-window on the day he pilfered the drivetrain from his dad's '55 Chevy wagon in 1970. The '55's green wheels are still attached to the rear end and the coupe got the 3-speed, too. The 265 V-8 was gifted to one Newark, California, neighbor, while the others only got more annoyed. Still a "work in progress" in this photo (originally gas welded together in 1967), it was sold in 1974. Carl and wife Donna said, "We just made the biggest mistake of our lives," as the new owner drove it away for $500, which they needed for a new dishwasher. Carl and Donna run a flathead dragster today, reminding us, "You don't get older, you just become a teenager in an older shell!" (Photo Courtesy Carl Lembke)

Middle and Bottom: It looks so clean through bloodshot rat eyes, but imagine Lance and Diane Sorchik's '34 badass parked next to a Ferrari red billetmobile when it debuted at the NSRA Nats East in 1986. "The reaction at York was good, but the reaction when we drove it to Pueblo for the Rocky Mountain Nationals was insane!" This was one of the brave pioneers who chewed a hole through the fence for today's rats to sneak through. Sorchik was an ink slinger at Rodder's Digest, *the only grassroots rodding magazine at the time. And yeah, Lance still has the coupe, unchanged (it still runs early Olds Rocket power through a 4-speed). These are recent shots from his home garage. He's still knocking out twisted hot rod art, too. (Photos Courtesy Lance Sorchik)

Rat rod momentum was already threatening to burst the dam when Rudy Rodriguez whipped up this '35 Ford truck for laughs and unwittingly supercharged the bobber truck craze. Rudy recalls, "I'd lost my house and everything else I owned, except that cab. I had to build something, so that was it." The bobber phenomenon spread to the point of uber-collector Ralph Whitworth buying "The Rudy Truck" to save for future generations to study. Go figure. Rudy Rodriguez shot these pics in his backyard while restoring the truck for Whitworth (it had already been sold and repainted before he found it). (Photos Courtesy Rudy Rodriguez)

CHAPTER 1: RAT EMBRYOS   13

Chapter 2

THE RESURGENCE OF UNFINISHED CARS

Tyler Souter's 1928 Ford Coupe.

—DRINKING KOOLAID WHILE DRIVING OVER CLIFFS

I**t's just physics: When the pendulum swings one way, it has to swing back the other way before finding the balance of middle ground.**

As rod and custom builders fed off one another's quest for excellence in craftsmanship, perfection began appearing on a regular basis, spawning a herd mentality that set up the hobby for a fierce backlash. This was especially apparent in the 1980s Street Rod world. At rod runs from coast to coast, flawless cars eventually became the norm and as the character of vintage tin was smoothed away in the name of cleanliness, the cars became lobotomized—faceless drones of conformity, just like the modern stockers they were intended to juxtapose. In hindsight, this was rodding's pivotal moment, as the repercussion came hard and loud: Hot rods had become ridiculously expensive lemmings, following the crowd right over the cliff.

At that point, the shift was on. Remember where we came from. Hot rods were meant to be Everyman's toys. Toys are fun to play with. Keep 'em realistic and expose their character so people can relate to them. Rejoice in the imperfections of these works in progress.

And most important, take 'em out of the box and play with them! These are active hands-on outlets for the creative process and should be driven as such.

Amen.

The next day, a few throwbacks gambled on sneaking their "unfinished" cars into some events, amusing Joe Public, who appreciated the educational value of exposed welds and other construction zone insights. The hot rods were back. Customs were sinister again. The pastel billets soon acquiesced to becoming minorities among minorities, themselves. A rodding renaissance had arrived and this time, everyone knew it should be savored before it became bastardized. Again.

In due time, profiteers capitalized on the lust for all that was pure and beautiful about homebuilt cars. But that's another story for another chapter. The keynote to this one is that history forgot to repeat one thing. This time around, although the focus had again shifted, the hot rod ethic remained. Tradition now stood alongside of acceptance to change. In spite of our sophomoric origins, we matured. Somewhat.

Mike Bermudez's '39 Ford pickup.
(Photo Courtesy Silas Warren)

CHAPTER 2: THE RESURGENCE OF UNFINISHED CARS

Jerry Fleck
Auto Repair Shop Owner
Ashland, Oregon
1924 Dodge Touring

Extensive research by veteran American film actor and historian George Leroy Tirebiter indicates this specimen could well be the very Dodge Touring driven by Joe Berkman's Mudhead character in the milepost teen culture film, *High School Madness*. Jerry Fleck isn't impressed: "I don't go to the movies much."

The tub body had been lying in Jerry's yard since being discovered in a vacant lot, years ago. Jerry thought it might make a nice planter some day. But he was too busy running his repair shop and playing with hot rods to worry about planters. During this period, Jerry was becoming disenchanted with hot rodding's pretentiousness. His blue-collar lifestyle wasn't blending with the polo shirt set. Then a story on rat rods in *Hot Rod* magazine re-sparked his interest. When Jerry tripped over a 1928 Buick frame that had been lying in a barn for 22 years, an idea was hatched. It was only an idea, until son-in-law Jerid Gunter got wind of it. Thirteen months later, it was a mobile wayback machine, delivering Jerry and Jerid to one wacky adventure after another, with no sign yet of slowing down.

A '59 Ford F-100 coughed up its steering and suspension for the cause. The period perfect engine was snatched from a snoozing '52 Olds sedan. A 1963 Ford truck transmission and 9-inch Ford rear end complete the drivetrain. The former yard sculpture was converted to a two-door, narrowed 4¾ inches from the doors back, and chopped windshield stanchions support a top frame erected from electrical conduit. Jerry and Jerid christened the tub with a fill-up of gasoline and a coat of dead bugs on the radiator shell and windshield.

Jerry says he's had more fun with this car than anything he's done since high school ("We'd poke holes in the muffler and have an instant hot rod!"). Jerid adds, "It wouldn't have happened without the chemistry we have; Jerry has the experience and I'm the thorn in his side, using my enthusiasm to push him to work on the car."

Whether or not Jerry's heap is an ex-movie star, he and George Tirebiter have lived somewhat parallel lives. When Jerry came home from Vietnam in 1970, Tirebiter received the Academy of Motion Picture Arts and Sciences' Department of Redundancy Department Award for his exposé of the Secret Code of Military Toughness in the 1958 Korean War epic, *Parallel Hell*.

"This is where the *fun* is in hot rodding today!"

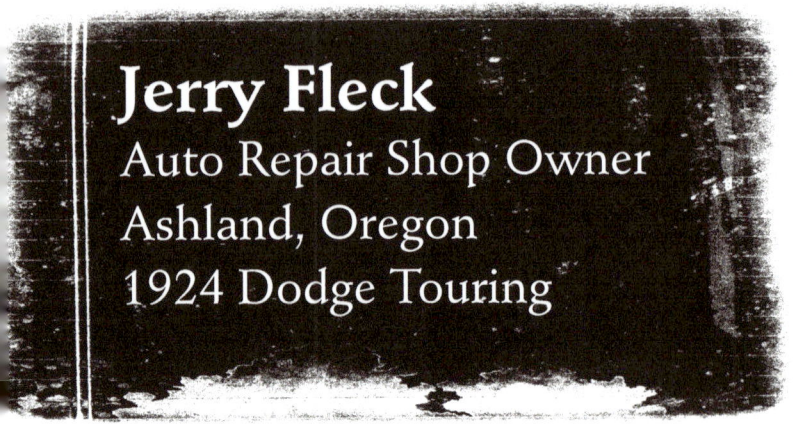

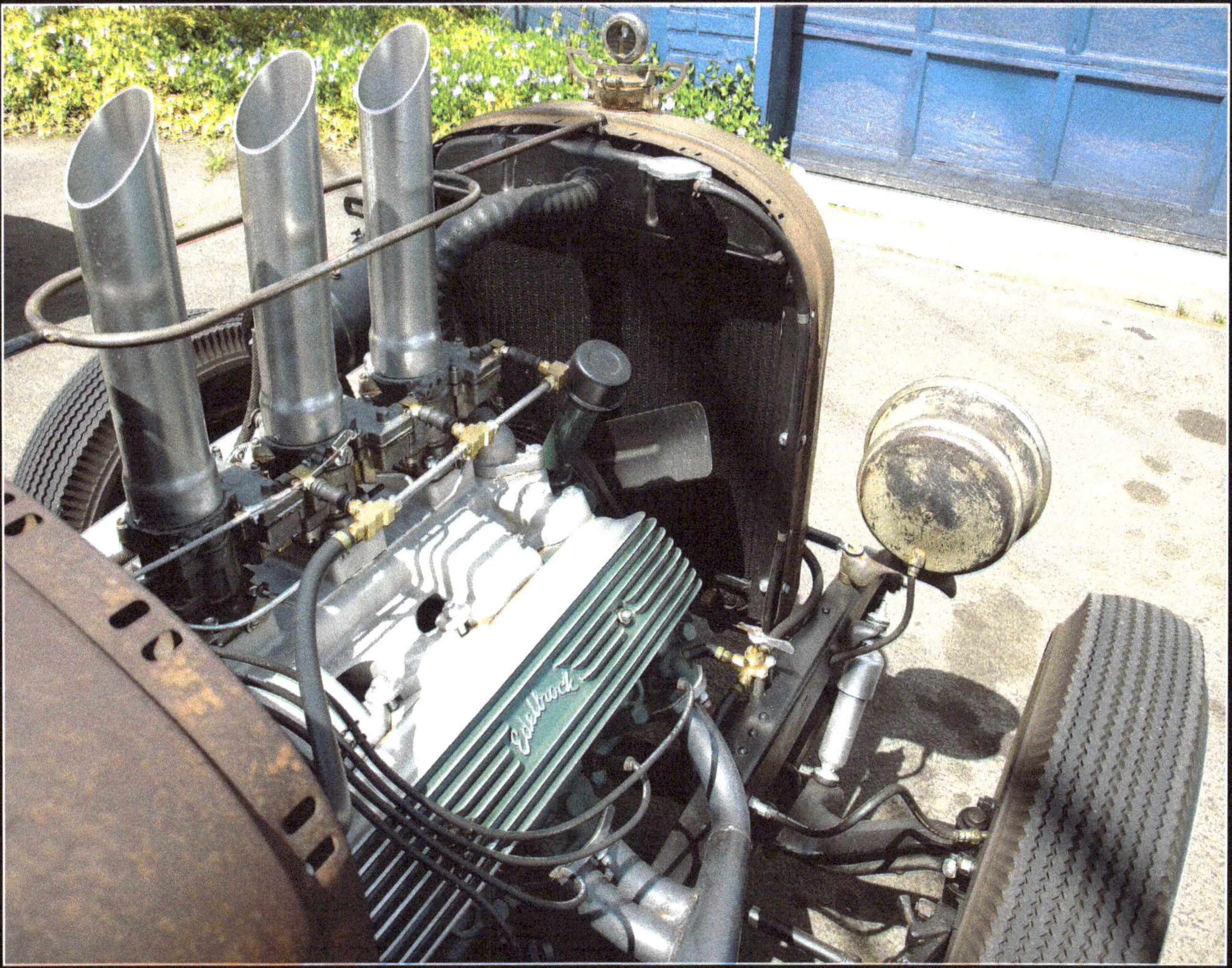

Huh? It's a fuel cooler now, previously an exhaust analyzer from Jerry's old Sun test center.

The '52 303-ci Olds was bored to 324 inches. Offenhauser manifold supports the Rochesters (with home-fabbed stacks) and directs the mix to stock heads, where it's expelled by home-brewed headers. The 1952 GMC radiator keeps temp at 180, tops. A mystery adaptor enables full-synchro shifts to the 3.50:1 9-inch Ford rear via 1963 Ford truck 3-speed.

Fleck headers feature volume adjustor collectors. Pretty clever and they work great.

The teensy **piston and rod** hanging from the mirror is from a **weed whacker.**

1972 Ford truck wheel sports antique wind-up clock horn button (it runs 12 hours per winding), plus there's a full complement of Stewart Warner gauges and some of Jerry's extensive beer bottle cap collection. The top, bench seat, and door panels wear black boat sail material from Ed's Upholstery (this is tough stuff!), while rear seat area is strictly for tool storage.

18 RAT RODS

Jerry's shop, where he does general repair work by day and crafts hot rods after hours. He and Jerid are putting together another Dodge Touring in there, right now. They get by with a "baby MIG" and delegate serious welds to Cory at Ashland Muffler. Jerry has been wrenching for a living since 1970, when he came home from Vietnam.

Ranier Morneau
Street Maintenance Worker
St. Paul, Minnesota
1927 Ford Coupe

When Ranier isn't plowing the snow packed streets of St. Paul, he's scorching them with motorcycles and hot rods or shredding them on his skateboard. Skateboarding is how he injured his leg a couple of Christmases ago and got sent home to rehabilitate. He was told he couldn't walk for six months. But Ranier had an intuitive insight about healing therapy. His plan was to get a jumpstart on his latest project to distract him from his mangled leg. "I used an office chair with casters to rest my bad leg on, so I could scoot around the shop." The response to this treatment was remarkable. Dragging around the busted leg became sport, while the focus stayed on the coupe. "I got it as a partially finished shell and perimeter frame. I Z'd the frame 3 inches in front and 9 inches out back."

Early Ford suspension and a GM drivetrain were installed and the body was chopped and channeled (6 inches each way). April showers were well underway when the body shell was finally lowered over the chassis. Ranier stepped back to check his work, oblivious to the welding burns on his oil-soaked leg cast. He couldn't stop grinning. But Ranier wasn't done yet. He still had another deadline to cross. "I was getting married in May. I had to finish the car so I could roll away with my new bride!"

Yeah, he made it. Ranier and wife Marisa blasted off to the wedding in the coupe. Daughters Nadia and Laila also enjoyed mega miles in the T, before it was sold to finance other projects. The Morneaus now use a spacious 1950 Merc as their "family hauler" and a Nailhead-powered A coupe is Ranier's latest thrill ride.

And the happy ending continues. The T's new owner, Sean Morgan (in Myrtle Beach, South Carolina), is now enjoying the healing powers of the "Broken Leg Coupe."

"I've really been enjoying the car!" says Sean. "I drive it to work and people don't know *what* to think! Ranier did a great job building this car. It goes straight as an arrow, has plenty of pep, stops good, and was built by a hobbyist in his garage, out of a love for this stuff!"

The *Journal of the American Medical Association* will likely plagiarize this story, so don't be surprised if a flat-black T jumps out at you, the next time you're absent mindedly thumbing through magazines in the waiting room. Just remember, you saw it here first. Effective physical therapy is as close as your own garage.

"I was mainly into the motorcycle scene, until it got all out of hand. Now I'm dedicated to the hot rod life. It's more family oriented and laid back."

(Photo Courtesy Scott Parkhurst)

He wisely kept the **tilt-out windshield** functional for summer days like this.

With a 6-inch chop and another 6 inches of channeling, Ranier knows how to get down! Garage-built, Z'd (3 inches), and kicked (9 inches) 2x3-inch frame helps. Black and gray (rattle can) color scheme enhances brushed-aluminum parts on engine, while restraint on chrome goodies keeps the package easy for the eyes to digest. Pinstriping is nice dessert. Ranier credits genetics for his skills. "My dad is a watch maker and mechanic. He can fix anything mechanical. I work on cars for fun. Sometimes I make money with it, but I like keeping it a hobby." (Photo Courtesy Scott Parkhurst)

The 1997 Vortech small-block was bored .030 inch over for 355 ci. The .480-inch-lift Crane flat-tappet hydraulic cam uses roller rockers and ZZ4 valvesprings to handle tall revs. Early heads were ported and polished by Hot Heads by Frank (in Minnesota) and use 2.02 valves. Speedway headers expel waste loudly and proudly ("I put in motorcycle baffles for long rides"). Under the velocity stack is a 600-cfm 4-barrel on an Edelbrock Performer Air Gap manifold. Jegs HEI provides zap. Vented cap on drag race thermostat housing eliminates steam pockets from low-mounted 1965 Mustang three-row radiator. Hayden 16-inch electric fan allows breezing through long red lights. The TH350 uses a B&M Stage 2 shift kit and 2200 stall converter to transfer the fun to a 9-inch Ford rear, loaded with a 3.23:1 limited slip pumpkin. Also note aluminum Corvair steering box hiding under header primaries and H.A.M.B. timing tag on smoothed firewall. (Photo Courtesy Scott Parkhurst)

Rats
are constantly in transition,
even when sitting at curbside!

Laying low in a city park until the coast is clear, the Morneaus savor tinkling of cooling headers and sizzling slicks, while the adrenaline subsides. Ahhh… (Photo Courtesy Marisa Morneau)

Facing Page: Ranier and Marisa, kicking the coupe around St. Paul. Note early version of headers and valve covers. (Photo Courtesy Marisa Morneau)

Clean and simple is the idea here and that always works. 1940 Ford axle and split wishbones support F-100 drums via Speedway reversed-eye spring. Pete and Jake's shocks clean up any extraneous chassis harmonics. It rolls on 15-inch Ford steelies wrapped with 670 Firestones in front and G-78 Goodyears out back. (Photo Courtesy Scott Parkhurst)

Stylish function reigns inside with quick-release silver-'flaked wheel (Cragar S/S cap horn button gets bonus points) and boat seats. Lokar shifter and 1953 Pontiac gauge cluster get the focus. Supplemental Sunpro gauges lurk on trans tunnel, while dual master cylinder hides under floorboard. Ranier found the stark interior a bit chilly, until adding Justin Wainner pinstriping. Late-model cup holders make it downright cozy. Speedway 12-gallon fuel tank emits just enough fumes to keep a good buzz on. (Photo Courtesy Scott Parkhurst)

His timing marks lined up perfectly. Tyler's generation has claimed rats to be *their* hot rods. He and dad Craig built several cars together, but Tyler's rat run began at the Turlock swap meet. "It was a rainy Sunday. I saw this coupe and was curious if I could even fit into it. I am over 6 feet tall and weigh 270 punds, but had to stretch to reach the pedals!" Bob Chandler (who is 6 feet, 4 inches tall) built the coupe to drag race in the Nostalgia Inliner class. Bob sold his old warrior to Tyler that day, knowing it was the beginning of a new chapter for all involved, none of whom could've guessed the story would still be unfolding, all these years later.

Tyler drove the coupe for a couple of years with Bob's old 1,588-cc Toyota four-banger harassing a nervous Toyota truck rear end with welded spider gears. He managed to have all that fun without any serious consequences and the coupe served its purpose well, introducing Tyler to a world viewed from the driver's side of a chopped windshield.

During those years behind the wheel, Tyler took copious mental notes, which he and Craig transferred to 3-D after tearing the coupe down for a rebuild. The rails were boxed, all chassis components were refurbished, and some "iffy" body panels were replaced. The Souters installed a new floor, fresh plumbing, and wiring. But question marks still hovered where motor and transmission mounts should be. "I wanted something different than the standard 350/350 recalls Tyler. He and Craig found the solution in a wrecked 1995 Mustang with a V-6/5-speed combo for $500, which only prompted another question: What to do about the conspicuous EFI throttle body? The answer was the same as it's been since rodding's first day—make something better yourself. So father and son concocted a homebrewed tri-power intake atop the bent six. Three 97s still work as good today as they did for Grandpa. Mounts were fabbed, the drivetrain was stabbed, and Tyler was grabbed, big time.

He's been flat-footing it ever since, ratting all over creation with his club, The Roadents. And Craig is also a regular on the scene. "He's my best friend," Tyler says of his dad. "We work and play together very well. There's nothing in life we can't do or overcome." So, the old drag coupe still carries a winning attitude.

"You can't have thin skin with rat rods. There's always someone telling you, 'That's wrong,' or 'That's stupid.' But at least I did something. Done or not, I'm driving it and not looking at it under a tarp in the garage. The best part is I got to build and enjoy it with my best friend, my dad. How cool is that!" (Photo Courtesy Rory Bright)

If only all father-son projects turned out like this.

Freshened chassis supports ex-drag car body, chopped 4 inches and channeled 2½ inches over boxed rails. A genuine Deuce radiator shell (with BBQ grille) lends some aero to the boxy body, along with frame horn apron, fabbed from gym locker. Tyler added eye candy in form of checkers and door art over natural patina. The 1937 Guide headlights and 1958 Edsel back-up lights (painted red) cap off the car's ends. Rear turn signals are still a mystery to Tyler. As usual, the rolling stock ties it all together: BFG 15x5.00s on 15x4 fronts and BFG 15x7.50s on 15x5 rears. (Photos Courtesy Dave Taylor, above; Rory Bright, below)

Tyler can exit a photo shoot with the best of 'em.

(Photo Courtesy Dave Taylor)

Power is courtesy of an unsuspecting 1995 Mustang that donated its 3.8-liter V-6/5-speed for Tyler's amusement. Bob Chandler's old Toyota rear (with welded spiders) is still holding up, somehow. Tyler and Craig fabbed the triple 97 intake and lake-style headers (with collector baffles) in their home shop. A Taurus distributor shoots the sparks. The radiator previously cooled a '74 Toyota. Tyler hasn't broken any parts or gotten any tickets, yet. (Photo Courtesy Rory Bright)

Indoor activities revolve around a 1984 Bronco seat, stitched up by Linda Johnson Upholstery. Eclipse gauges in a Deuce dash constitute entertainment center, enhanced by circa 1964 Indiana drive-in speakers. The 1937 GM heater and mid-1950s Star Manufacturing swamp cooler ("Just add water!") provide climate control. Skate-punk tennies bring shifter and e-brake boots up to date. The 1969 MG wheel tops off the fun center interior. Swanky digs, compared to coupe's race car days. (Photo Courtesy Rory Bright)

Portrait of an ex-drag racer in twilight. It seems to have made the transition back to street duty with attitude intact. And there's some serious genetic mojo at work here. (Photo Courtesy Tyler Souter)

Here's a guy who might otherwise be lying on the couch, playing a video game. But thanks to a proper upbringing, Tyler is out on the streets with his gang of hoodlums (the Roadents Car Club) cheating death and/or jail. Rest easy, America. (Photo Courtesy Rory Bright)

CHAPTER 2: THE RESURGENCE OF UNFINISHED CARS

Chuck Motzko
Photographer
Delano, Minnesota
1929 Ford Pickup

The car on the cover of this book is merely the latest offering in the long parade of madcap hot rods rumbling out of Chuck Motzko's home garage. Some previous highlights include the '53 Chevy "Tin Woodie" wagon (his first car) that he wrapped around a tree, then learned to do sheet-metal work on; a '59 Ford, so nice that, "When I waxed it, it would actually shine!"; the Y-block-powered VW Bug on a Model T frame; a 392-ci Hemi with dual quads powered his VW van, "back in my hippy days"; a blown big-block '40 Willys. And of course, there was the Postal Service Jeep with yet another big-block Chevy engine. Are you picking up on what he's laying down?

So this Model A truck just fits right into the festivities. Chuck explains, "I found a rickety old Model A pickup body and I had to have it. The previous owner had chopped it, but stopped for some reason." Chuck took over from there, scratch-building a frame and strapping on the ubiquitous early Ford suspenders up front, while a 9-inch Ford swinging on four-bars, coil-overs, and a Panhard bar anchors the rear. Chuck conjured up a small-block Chevy/6-speed combo to fill the space between the rails. Chuck and wife Linda were vacationing in France, when a Citroën single-spoke steering wheel caught his eye and "I took the idea home with me." That inspired the wide-open-minded approach to the rest of the interior. The waist-high exterior speaks for itself, with pinstripes by Bo Huff, Jr. as an exclamation point.

I crossed paths with "The Chuck Truck" at a Gopher State Timing Association event, where it definitely left a mark on me—the doctors say the header burns and tire marks should heal, eventually. Meanwhile, Chuck is back home with Linda ("She puts up with my busy schedule and messy garage"), thrashing on a right-hand-drive Model T Ford. That sounds about right. And after that?

"The Chuck Truck" has a gift for finding trouble, even on this rural driveway (I can't say more without lawyers present). The unique headlighting reveals a warmth not found on many rods. Stance, headers, and radical chop are exaggerated by high-flying foxtail. Chuck has a nice sense of balance. (Photo Courtesy Scott Parkhurst)

You just can't beat the timeless, functional beauty of OEM early-Ford suspension, but note the disc brakes hiding behind the 'stones on 1935 wires—safety is our friend, in the real world. Chuck went with a 1953 Ford truck steering box, continuing the "mostly trad" theme. Dig the tri-tailed aeroplane on the drilled axle and the yellow-bulbed, purple-lensed T headlights. (Photo Courtesy Scott Parkhurst)

(Photo Courtesy Scott Parkhurst)

"When you have nothing but a **rusty car**, you have to stretch your mind and your creativeness."

Open-air touring in a closed-cab truck? Yes! Hung art and a 6-speed sculpture on display generate gallery-like ambiance. Air-ride seating may seem pretentious for a rat, but hey, the alternative is . . . hemmoroids! Ewww! Chuck says, "You sit so low in the truck that your eyes are at windowsill level. You drive, looking through the steering wheel." Wilwood pedals operate same-make binders and Centerforce clutch. (Photo Courtesy Scott Parkhurst)

How much adventure can you find, with 14 gallons of gas to burn?

Top: When Chuck discovered the mono-spoke steering wheel on a Citroën, he swore the truck would have one and he wasn't bluffing (note the quick-release pin). Chuck relaxes with some reading material (Summit gauge cluster), while lucky passengers admire his bungee cord collection. (Photo Courtesy Scott Parkhurst) *Middle:* Three deuces on the Packard V-8—wait, that's a small-block Chevy, wearing what appears to be cast-iron valve cover adapters. Where does he find this stuff? Very funny, Charles! Actually, it's a 350, spinning a 400 crank, making 383 cubes. Tri-power and early zoomie-style headers help the mouse-in-a-rat make enough steam to pull the little trucklet around effortlessly. The Z-28 6-speed keeps the muscle available in any situation and a 9-inch Ford rear end relays it to the asphalt. Chuck says, "All I know about the gear ratio is it's pretty high. I only use about half of the gears to stay with traffic!" (Photo Courtesy Scott Parkhurst) *Bottom:* Despite plasma-cut backlight imagery, the topless phone booth is no artful dodger. Chuck embraces all challenges, as he heads out on safari for kicks. There's a 14-gallon fuel cell lurking under the vinyl bed cover (the gas gauge is 1920s-style wooden stick). Close look reveals backup light tucked in behind tire: another nice touch. Bon voyage, Chuck! We'll see you out there, somewhere. (Photo Courtesy Scott Parkhurst)

Zach Kurth
Bartender
Zimmerman, Minnesota
1931 Ford Tudor

If you haven't built your own rat yet, here's Zach Kurth's secret down-and-dirty recipe. But you better panic—you're missing out on all the fun!

Being goal oriented, Zach planned his work and worked his plan. The primary objective was to build a car within his budget to drive on the *Hot Rod* Power Tour. Step one was teaming up with old pal "Big Daddy" Don Kreger from Elk River. "Without him, this car would not have been. We set out with 17 weeks and three grand in cash and this is what we got. Most people have more money in their TVs than I have in this car. It's very real and runs and drives so nice." Sounds like a success already. How'd they pull it off?

Zach and Don already had some Model A experience and connections, so that's where they started, with a crusty frame and enough body parts to mock up this Tudor. The rails were cleaned up, kicked in the ass (a 16-inch rear kick-up!), and Z'd 3 inches up front, ensuring a snake-like final stance. A 9-inch Ford rear end from a '78 van was used to locate the rear wheels and a dropped tube axle did the same up front. When the general proportions and wheelbase were decided on, they connected the dots and—*voilà!* Instant funmobile!

Okay, there's more to it than that, but the rest of the pieces basically fell into place. For example, when a large opening between the firewall and radiator was discovered, they filled it with a 350 Chevy, backed with a 200R4 overdrive automatic. Body mounts were fabbed and the chopped Tudor shell was channeled over the chassis. Once plumbed and wired, Zach and Big Daddy registered for the *Hot Rod* Power Tour, filled the tank, and aimed the A-bomb at America.

"No spare tire, no tools—we just hit the road to see how well we really did. We were clocked at 110 mph with a radar gun—not smart and I can't really explain how I walked away from that ticket. I have just over 13,000 miles on it now. The car spins about 20 mpg all day, every day." The sedan ran Power Tour without incident, except for upstaging some pretty high-zoot rods along the way. Also, "We passed over forty broken-down cars on the Tour—that feeling was priceless." Look for Zach to repeat on this year's Tour, too—he just can't get enough of that road rash stuff. Zach's bottom line: "We put a car on the road that every income bracket can afford." Henry Ford may have said it first, but now Zach Kurth can say it, too.

"Rain, sleet, shit, or shine, I'll drive it any time! There are other rats out there that I wouldn't trust to go to the mailbox." (Photo Courtesy Scott Parkhurst)

Your basic 350 Chevy (Olds valve covers are just there for snickers) was updated with a Hitech Motorsports cam and Pertronix ignition, while the compression was set at 10:1. The custom headers were outfitted with cutouts that tuck underneath for freeway use. A 200R4 and 3.73:1 gears enable endless burnouts, hard charges, and lazy freeway miles. A well-thought-out mix of torque band and gearing for the bucks. (Photo Courtesy Scott Parkhurst)

A **Moto Guzzi** motorcycle gas tank makes for a *snarky* air scoop!

Left: Zach knew he was dialing long distance on this build, so plenty of opulent accoutrements were designed into the cabin. The filled-top insert covers a headliner of 1x3-inch pine slats, while wooden door panels were previously outhouse walls—features one would demand of any luxury sedan. Luxurious handcrafted seating and imported carpet (from somewhere) complete private-club lodge ambiance. (Photo Courtesy Scott Parkhurst) *Right:* Zach says the paint is by Mother Nature. "I would paint it, but you don't want to piss off anyone's mother." A 3-inch chop and 4-inch channel combine with slammed chassis for menacing stance that makes lesser cars leak fluids upon sighting the 1931. The 1950 Farmall M radiator shell adds elegant touch of distinction. 14x5.60 front and 15x6.70 rear whitewalls on green steelies are offset by fine pinstripes, further enhancing the Model A's sophistication. (Photo Courtesy Scott Parkhurst)

Left: Pockmarked sheet metal reminds me of nerve-wracking high school dates. The character oozes from every inch of this sedan. (Photo Courtesy Scott Parkhurst) *Right:* Home-brewed 2x3-inch rear rails kick up a whopping 16 inches worth of drop. The triangulated four-bars locate the 9-inch Ford housing. Partially boxed A-bone rails were Z'd 3 inches at firewall to complement Speedway dropped-tube front axle, defining stance. The 2,500-pound air bags keep everything above the potholes. The budget took a hit on safety gear, but Zach didn't complain: "It had to be as safe as you can make a '31 Ford." That explains the S-10 disc brakes in front and 11-inch drums in back. Nice prioritizing, Zach! Here's evidence of good planning: Zach longhauled Power Tour 2008, drama free. "It's very real and runs and drives so nice." (Photo Courtesy Scott Parkhurst)

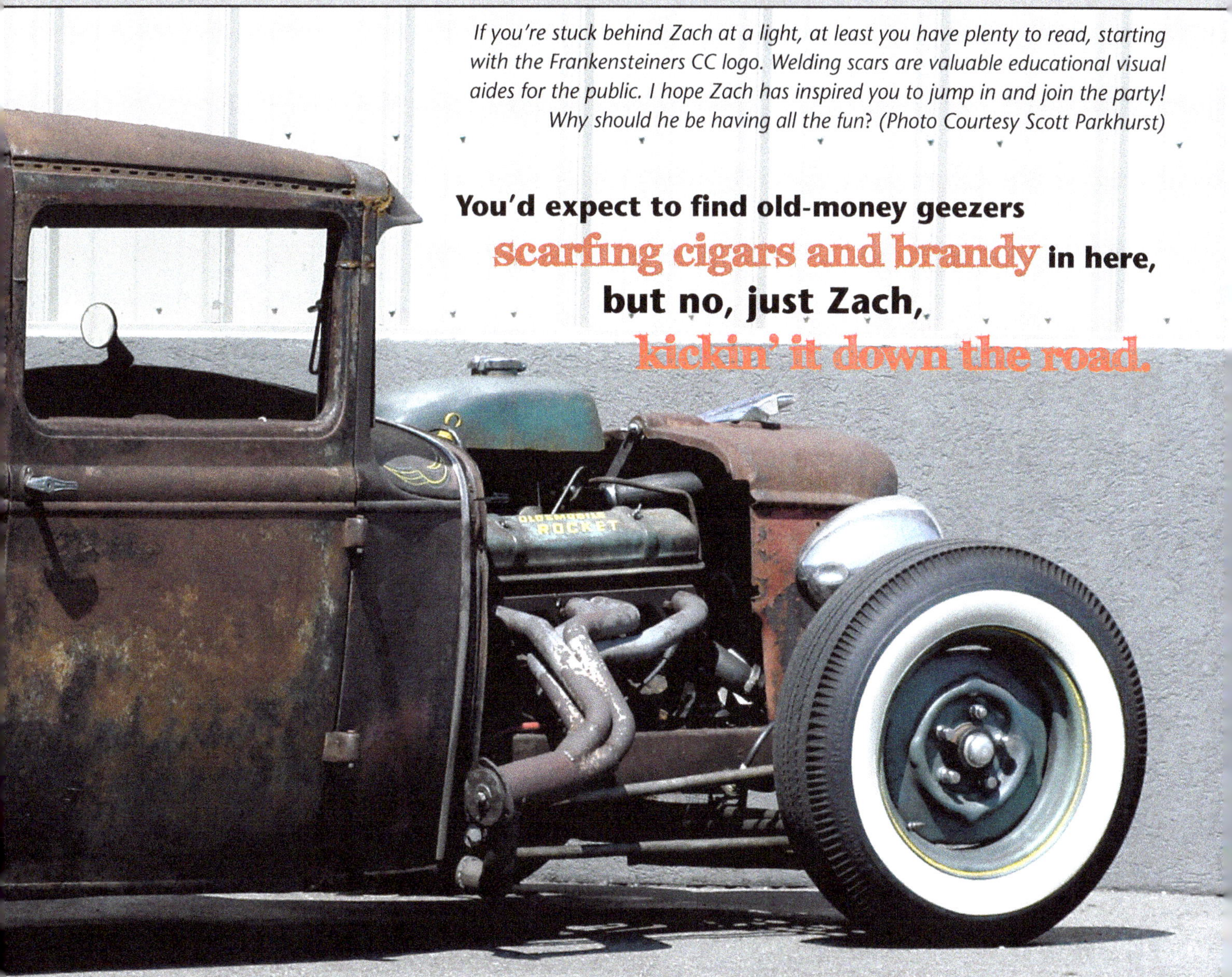

If you're stuck behind Zach at a light, at least you have plenty to read, starting with the Frankensteiners CC logo. Welding scars are valuable educational visual aides for the public. I hope Zach has inspired you to jump in and join the party! Why should he be having all the fun? (Photo Courtesy Scott Parkhurst)

You'd expect to find old-money geezers **scarfing cigars and brandy** in here, but no, just Zach, **kickin' it down the road.**

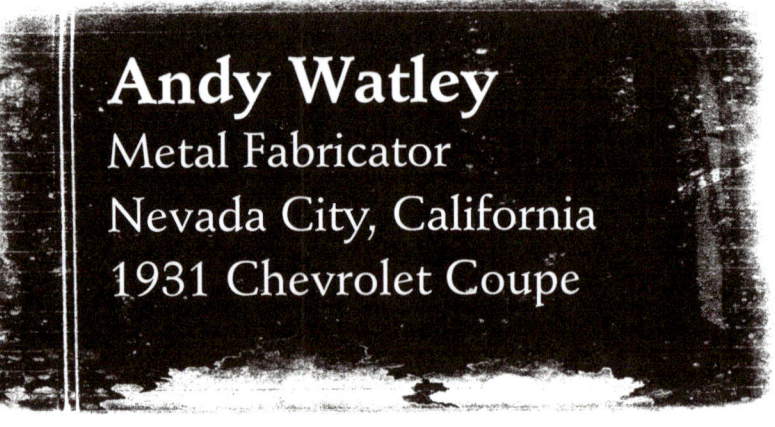

Andy Watley
Metal Fabricator
Nevada City, California
1931 Chevrolet Coupe

This is Andy's first time at bat and he knocked it clean out of the park. Apparently, nobody told Andy to approach his first project with caution. He just went at it like he was killing snakes and garnered a stunning result. Oh, and another thing nobody told Andy before he dove into the stovebolt: "Chevy cars in the 1930s had a lot of wood in them, so I removed it all and replaced it with steel tubing." At that point, he was ready to begin getting ready to begin. He had a body shell and a radiator shell.

Andy's first move was establishing a 2x4-inch platform. Then he just filled in the spaces that didn't look like a '31 Chevy. "I got a used 350 Chevy and a rebuilt Turbo 400 transmission. Later, I found a 9-inch Bronco rear axle and I was ready to start. I took some 3-inch masking tape and laid out the chop and started cutting. Then I put it back together. The body was channeled 4 inches over the frame." Simple, right? Besides a body structure reinforced with wood, another Chevy quirk was parallel front leaves, which Andy deftly dodged by using early Ford front suspension. He cut to the chase out back with coil-overs and homemade ladder bars.

The result is not only an impressive freshman effort, but a highly functioning visual homage to the dirt trackers of yore. Andy's father-in-law Fred Vanocco ran those cars back in the day and his tales of Friday night dirt clod fights were a major influence on Andy. The little Chevy is a fast but reliable street car that could no doubt hold its own on the track as well.

"I started with the idea of a low-budget rat rod, but by the time I was done, I had a very high-end custom rat. Now that the car is done, the family and I take it to every car show we can and we have a lot of fun with it!" That must be so satisfying. Or not. "I'm really looking forward to my next build."

Since finishing his Chevy, Andy has knocked out three more rods for happy customers. He's now hoping to become a full-time builder and is already rounding third on his way to home plate. It's probably wise to stay out of his way and just let him run.

"In the beginning, we all bolted on silly crap for something to laugh at. But now we're going to more traditional, functional hardware and less gimmicky ornamentation."
(Photo Courtesy Dave Taylor)

Top: Andy brings the dirt-track ethos to the street with nerf bars all around and a squaty stance evoking a drift out of turn four. GMs came with parallel leaves, but Wasley went buggy, using a 4-inch dropped S&W axle on hairpins to keep up tradition, keep down ride height. The 1953 Ford juice brakes mount 17-inch 1933 Ford wires on all fours, wrapped with Sears Allstate 5.50 rubber. Steering is a 1953 F-100. Andy, what kind of headlights are those? "Big, old, and still a mystery." (Photo Courtesy Dave Taylor) Bottom: The 1940 Chevy blue dot taillights hang on for dear life below sculpted chevron wings. The third brake light adds stylish safety. Ladder bars, Panhard rod, and aluminum QA1 coil-overs prop up the 9-inch Ford housing. Again, is it just me, or does the coupe always appear to be in motion, even when turned off? (Photo Courtesy Dave Taylor)

CHAPTER 2: THE RESURGENCE OF UNFINISHED CARS

"I decided to suicide the doors, but leave the hinges and handles in their normal spots to throw people off." It worked. I nearly sprained my connectezoids, double-taking this freakshow! (Photo Courtesy Dave Taylor)

Andy made a *surprise exit* at this photo-op.

Obsessive detailing run amok makes for sanitized operating room. Highlights include de rigueur Speedway sprint car wheel, Dolphin gauges (note tach sunk into drive-in speaker), steroid-enhanced e-brake, Lokar shifter, and console built from Schwinn bike tank (check surfer foot-dimmer switch). More drive-in-speaker castings (mounted behind seats) use upgraded speakers connected to iPod dock. Army tent material covers door panels and top insert. (Photos Courtesy Dave Taylor)

Thanks for keeping our dirt-track memories alive, guys. Drive accordingly! (Photo Courtesy Dave Taylor)

Fred and Andy, appearing decidedly suspicious with the coupe they created to raise holy hell.

The end. Roll credits. Special thanks to Roadents Car Club, pix by Dave Taylor, soundtrack by General Motors, and Fred Vanocco. (Photo Courtesy Dave Taylor)

CHAPTER 2: THE RESURGENCE OF UNFINISHED CARS

Don Moyer III
Retired Honda Service Tech
Cleveland, Ohio
1936 Ford Five-Window Coupe

If the name seems familiar, you've been paying attention. Don's dad (Don Moyer II) put the Moyer name on the map decades ago, with the infamous *Lazy 8* '31 roadster (its history goes back to 1948), which now resides in Don III's garage. Don savors "fond memories of riding in the rumble seat as a youngster, hearing The Beach Boys on the new eight-track tape player."

He's been twirling wrenches since age 10, when he tore into an AMC Gremlin, which he still owns (how many of us still have our first car?). That's where his automotive momentum began and it continues to roll. "I'm still learning . . ."

When a family friend brought this '36 coupe to Don's garage for a build-up after finding it flattened under a fallen tree, the task seemed so daunting that the customer decided selling it to Don would be the easy way out. Don and wife Michelle declared the five-window to be the perfect daily driver candidate, since it carried more armor to guard against texting SUV drivers than thin-skinned Model Ts and As. "And I wanted my kids to know what a rumble seat was," adds Don.

"The plan was to keep it simple and cheap—a car I didn't have to yell at the kids to be careful around . . . as much." The body was punched back into shape, blasted, and primed. A 1953 flathead V-8 was assembled with all the beefy stuff and bolted up to the original 1936 drivetrain, as per tradition. Wiring, plumbing, lights, and glass were installed and a license plate was hung. Don considered the coupe "done" when he converted the trunk to a rumble seat, complete with the original rumble seat cushions from the *Lazy 8* roadster! Some typical minor kinks were worked out and the Moyers had a daily driver. "Groceries, parts store, drive the kids to softball or baton twirling. I'll come out of the grocery store and find people standing by the car, looking at it. It's always the same conversation:

'Nice start—when are you going to finish it?'
'It's done.'
'What a shame—it could be so nice, blah, blah, blah.'
'I agree, it would be nice—too nice to be in a grocery store parking lot. Then you wouldn't get to enjoy it on this nice day.'
Most of the time, they agree."

"I think the rat rod can be credited with the resurgence of traditional hot rods. Street rodding was going mega-cubic-dollars. Along came rat rodding, where limited funds and unlimited imagination, coupled with the ease of building these cars, came into vogue. Kind of like hot rodding in the beginning." (Photo Courtesy Don Moyer)

Striking a swanky pose outside an infamous local establishment (do not go in there unarmed), the coupe is stylin', especially considering it lay smashed under a large tree for many years. Don is using fiberglass fenders for the moment, but has some steel ones on the way. The top was filled when he got the car, so he's leaving it, for now. (Photo Courtesy Don Moyer)

At a Slick Devil club meeting, pal Curly's '55 Pontiac gets the limelight, while the '36 stands by, knowing it may have to make a full-throttle exit on a moment's notice. (Photos Courtesy Don Moyer)

Yes, Don is one Slick Devil.

Women love rats, especially with lavish interiors like this!

Don snapped model Katie, over the photog's shoulder during a recent magazine shoot. Predictably, the swap meet bucket seats and gauges (Don is swapping in a more period info center soon) have dazzled her into a case of the vapors. If Katie looks over her shoulder, she'll see a plush T-bird rear seat beckoning her. No woman alive can resist that! (Don calls it The Lovenasium.) (Photo Courtesy Don Moyer)

The 1953 side-valve came with the car. It now boasts a Merc crank, stereo 97s on an Offenhauser intake, and Offy heads. Don has been tuning it to perfection for carefree driving ("Keep it simple and cheap"). The remainder of drivetrain is stock '36 Ford. The biggest job so far has been re-coring the radiator. (Photo Courtesy Don Moyer)

Hittin' the bricks of Painesville, Ohio, on a crisp autumn morning. Can you smell the coffee and 90-wt? Where's that donut shop? (Photo Courtesy Don Moyer)

The trusty '36 catches its breath before heading out on its next mission. Rumble seat conversion was top priority. Don is easy to find around the Cleveland area, just listen for the flatty barking down the street. (Photo Courtesy Don Moyer)

Troy Nicolas
Millwright/Welder
Penticton, B.C., Canada
1940 Ford Pickup

Deep inside every hot rodder are billions of hyperkinetic molecules spinning at fierce velocity to support a unique genetic code distinguished by the ultra rare "Y" and "Y-not" chromosomes. Discovered in recent government funded studies at Friends University of Central Kansas, the anomaly is currently believed to be the only plausible explanation for today's rodders asking, "Why not ignore 100 years of technology and do it like Dad did?" Don't ask how I gained access to this classified information.

Luckily for Troy Nicolas, he inherited a pretty nice pair of genes from his dad Gary, a lifelong hot rodder. By age four, Troy was mystifying his folks by identifying every car on the road (including tech specs). That led to a muscle car infatuation and ultimately, his 1,000-hp '92 Mustang (already a 9-second street sweeper, now shooting for 8s with a huffed and stroked small-block). Meanwhile, dad Gary had been on Troy to join him in some vintage tin fun, but it wasn't until Gary passed away in 2005 that Troy was finally ready to get rusty. "I've been bitten by the old car bug ever since. Better late than never, I suppose!"

Troy was actually searching for a 1950s sled project when he came across the '40 pickup online. "The truck was originally from Texas, but I purchased it from a guy in Langley, B.C., who bought it from someone at the Portland swap meet." Rats tend to network through an underground maze, for sure. "It was chopped already, but the work was not to my liking." So Troy tore into the top and worked his way straight to the bottom of the truck. When the sparks, smoke, and dust finally settled, the '40 was seriously chopped and channeled over the original frame and suspension, with a 1956 Buick drivetrain jutting up between the front fenders' cleavage.

"It's so rewarding to see something transform right in front of you, from your own vision. The truck makes tons of power and is very light, which makes it a blast to run on the street. It looks rough, but it passed the safety inspection with no issues, which really pisses off the local fuzz! It rattles and shakes like crazy and people just stare when they see it coming. I run this truck all the time, with my wife Carolina and English Bulldog Vernon riding shotgun."

Gary would be so proud. Sounds like the right pair of genes can take you anywhere you want to go. Why not, indeed . . .

Rattling into any car gathering in this thing is an event in itself.

"It gets more attention than the high-dollar cars. I think it's because people can relate to it, due to the fact that it's not expensive and it's very simple." For his next trick, Troy will Gasserize his dad's old '55 Dodge pickup. (Photo Courtesy Byron Kane)

Sneak peek at the 1940's inner workings reveals 1965 Falcon seats, Superior wheel on stock column (shortened 6 inches), and Mr. Gasket shifter crowned with crystal knob. A Painless wiring kit zaps the truck into the modern (12-volt) era. Basic function rules in here. (Photos Courtesy Byron Kane)

Currently wrapped in DP-90, Troy is considering a coat of brown Hot Rod Flatz. He'll keep the HID headlights and LED taillights, though (Troy's only concession to modern tech). Ditto for the red steelies. Door art by Heath Anthony at Hopeless Graphics was freehanded with wrecking yard paint pens. (Photo Courtesy Byron Kane)

Besides the sinister stance, the other star of the show is the 1956 Nailhead, gulping fresh air in front of God and everybody. Internally stock (except for a rowdy Comp Cams stick), the 322-incher runs an Edelbrock 4-barrel on an Eelco intake and stock exhaust manifolds with Smitty glasspacks. The valve covers are powdercoated. A Valiant radiator with electric fan keeps it happy. The Buick mill is backed with a Dynaflow trans for shiftless operation, so Troy can keep both hands on the wheel! 3.73:1 gears in the 10-bolt posi keeps the torque handy. (Photo Courtesy Byron Kane)

CHAPTER 2: THE RESURGENCE OF UNFINISHED CARS 45

"It's kind of funny how I appreciate **all the rattles, wandering, and poor brakes** that came from the factory in the 1940s and 1950s.

Tasteful grille ornament evokes aura of elegance, defining classic status. (Photo Courtesy Byron Kane)

Memorize this mug. Troy appears to be contemplating his next move here. Expect it to be high risk and irresistibly fun. (Photo Courtesy Byron Kane)

"I would've loved to have grown up back in the days when life was simpler and innocent, and there were tons of these cool rides to be had." (Photo Courtesy Byron Kane)

CHAPTER 2: THE RESURGENCE OF UNFINISHED CARS 47

Colin Zimmerman
Mechanic/Bodyman
Winnipeg, Manitoba, Canada
1949 Plymouth Four-Door Sedan

None of us knows how long our fuse is. So when life gets weird, we just ride it out to Point B and end up wiser for the experience. That approach worked out pretty well for Colin Zimmerman, owner-operator of this sinister Mayflower sled. It's a low-buck funmobile and more. The Plymouth is also Colin's daily driver and a daily reminder that we can't truly know joy without also knowing some pain. Such is life.

Colin was brought up in a tight family. His dad is a mechanic and auto shop instructor, who passed his skills on to his son early. Colin recalls, "I used to help him in the garage, putting tools away, cleaning parts and stuff." That led to dirt bikes, go-karts, and eventually, a slammed and primered '61 GMC shortbed in the high school parking lot. Colin spent the next twenty-some years working as a licensed mechanic and bodyman at various shops around the area. His lifelong dream was to own both a hot rod and a custom, so when he scored a Model T coupe on the cheap, he was halfway home. Wife Nadel wanted in on the fun and the Zimmermans bought (fellow Riff Raff club member) Brent Hoitink's Plymouth. At that point, the Zimmermans had a hot rod and a custom, making for a potential one-two punch at the burger joints. But the marriage eventually went sour, as sometimes happens, and Colin found himself the caretaker of a 4-door Plymouth.

"She picked it out. This wouldn't be my first choice for a sled build, but it's what I had," is Colin's take on the scenario. Upon Nadel's exit, Colin personalized the Mopar by throwing every bodywork trick he knew at it and stepping up the drivetrain and suspension to early-1950s equipment. It's still a work in progress ("Always will be"), but is distinctly Colin's now. "I'm a GM guy, but I'm digging the Mopar education. And there aren't many like mine around. It really stands out among all the Mercs and Chevys. And being a four-door makes it more of a challenge." The transformation from crotchety slug to sleek custom is extraordinary. More impressive yet is how Colin came to accept it for what it is, making peace with himself in the process. The T coupe is now coming together and Colin's next challenge will be choosing which set of keys to grab.

Colin thanks all of the Riff Raff club members ("Especially Brent Hoitink!") and his family for their help and support.

"Anybody can throw his wallet at a car. Doing it this way is more real to me. If you work hard enough, your dreams can come true." (Photo Courtesy Cam Zimmerman)

Above (left and right): When Colin inherited the Mayflower, he deemed it the healthiest pain medication he could take. The body was stripped to bare metal, the top was re-chopped, the three-piece front fenders were molded into single units, and the rears were welded to the body. The hood was nosed and peaked (although hood ornament survived), grille bars were shortened, and parking lights filled. The headlights were frenched using Mercury Meteor frames. A "cleaner" 1952 Dodge deck lid was swapped on and both iconic ribbed bumpers were tucked in. The rear door handles were shaved and the windshield and backlight were flush mounted. Tying the package together are bias-ply 3-inch whitewall tires and full Moon discs. Good medicine, indeed. Colin feels better than James Brown now. (Photos Courtesy Cam Zimmerman) *Left:* The original flathead six was using a cane, so Colin swapped in this space-age 1954 model. He performed a valve job, installed fresh gaskets and a Volare carb to make it sing like a Singer. It's hooked to a 3-speed overdrive transmission. This drivetrain will remain through 2011, then be replaced with overhead V-8 power (Colin's leaning toward a 318/727 package). Meanwhile, he gets to experience occasional six-banger quirkiness. (Photo Courtesy Cam Zimmerman) *Below:* Yes, the interior is a construction zone, but Colin's digging the relaxed ambiance of the Plymouth's original art deco presentation. Does he get points for fuzzy dice and a necker knob? Your call. (Photo Courtesy Cam Zimmerman)

Brent Hoitink owned the MoCar previously. It was a scabby blue and completely covered with graffiti. A real grin maker, but nowhere near the car bomb it is here. The view from a passing Chevy reveals result of Colin-made 3-inch blocks to droop the tail and swapped-in 1954 Dodge springs for a 2-inch dive up front. He's planning a bagged S-10 clip, which is a solid upgrade, but I'm fine with the vintage approach. Alas, rats are in a constant state of evolution, lest things get stagnant, you know. (Photo Courtesy Cam Zimmerman)

Does this look like the perfect car and driver match, or what?

Looks to me like things worked out just right for Colin. (Photo Courtesy Cam Zimmerman)

Photo shoots can be tedious affairs. When boredom strikes, primal urges take over. Fellow Riff Raff CC members Charlene and Kyle Ross own the '54 Chevy, also powered by a six-cylinder/automatic (with stripes by Riff Raffer Von Knob). The participants gave me conflicting reports of the outcome, but Colin got the last word, "When I add the V-8 next winter, mine will be way faster!" (Photo Courtesy Cam Zimmerman)

Life is sweet, eh?

After the photo shoot, the Mayflower ferries Colin back to Winnipeg and the daily grind at the shop. He has a '27 coupe waiting for him there. (Photo Courtesy Cam Zimmerman)

Chuck Barr
Shop Manager
Portland, Oregon
1950 Mercury Coupe

Chuck was born in Michigan, three days after his Merc rolled off the assembly line there. His earliest memory is watching his dad and uncle crew on a jalopy racer at the dirt track. The family moved to southern California in 1963 and Chuck's automotive lifestyle shifted into hyperdrive. "Our place was 4 miles from Lions Drag Strip and 5 miles from Ascot. Wild Willy Borsch was our neighbor. I never had a chance *not* to be a car guy!" Chuck hustled cars and parts through high school. He still has the '48 Thames he bought in 1966, but Chuck's Holy Grail was the elusive 1949–1951 Mercurys that scraped through his dreams every night.

1974 found Chuck married and living in Oregon, with dream intact. "I'd drive around, looking for cars. After a few months, I found the Merc, sitting under a lilac bush with no hood and a flathead full of water. $200 later, it was home. After two days' work and $50 in parts, it was driving."

Chuck enjoyed some seat time in the Merc, while collecting parts for the build. "On New Years Day of 1980, I decided to start chopping it. Only one problem—I couldn't weld! I had the "How to Chop a Merc" issue of *Rod & Custom* taped to the wall and a hacksaw and saber saw ready. No welder, no cutoff wheels, no brains!" The cavalry arrived in the form of the McClanahan brothers, Carl and Dennis. Chuck explains, "Carl's my best friend. The McClanahans taught me to weld, do body work, and make the Merc into my pride and joy."

Part One of the plan was now in place. "It had to be chopped to be a Merc!" And Part Two? "It had to have an old-school Hemi!" The original flathead served its time and even won a few races, but was replaced by a big-block Chevy in 1986. Then Chuck met northwest flathead and Hemi guru Earl Floyd, who hooked him up with a genuine 392-ci Hemi. After much head scratching, the elephant motor now pulls an overdrive stick in the sled that had occupied Chuck's head for years.

In the process, Chuck realized his potential too, working his way from his garage to developing a fiberglass body program at Old Chicago Street Rods, to Steve's Auto Restorations, where he now serves as General Manager. "My dream job!" Rat dreams always come true, when car and owner live parallel lives.

"I love what rats have done for the hobby. Getting stuck on just what is a 'rat rod' is no different than 'street rod,' 'hot rod,' 'resto mod,' or whatever. I know the difference. Car guys should stick together. The hobby has greater problems than car names or classifications." (Photo Courtesy Chris Clark)

Top: There's more than a chop-and-slam happening here. Frenched Monte Carlo headlights, radiused corners on doors and deck, expert stainless work on window trim, custom skirts, nosing, and decking all add up to quintessential Merc dressing. Attitude, beauty, and function are all present and accounted for. Stock grille, bumpers, and other trim denote mild custom specs, but the chop drops the Merc into the full-custom box. Is it mildly wild, or wildly mild? Rats don't even acknowledge such questions. (Photo Courtesy Chris Clark) *Bottom:* Chuck needed no help with inspiration, confiding, "I'd gone to the premier of *American Graffiti* in California and loved the Pharaohs' Merc. Then, I saw the Sam Barris Merc in person." And that was that. Chuck and the McClanahan brothers cut 4 inches from the top, pancaked it 2 inches, laid the backlight down, and elected to leave the B-pillars upright. Chuck acknowledges, "A lot of people tell me I should've slanted them, but they don't know this is easier. I like it." Either way, nothing else can lurk like a Merc. Chuck runs sans plaque in these shots, but is a card-carrying Dukes club member. (Photo Courtesy Chris Clark)

Left: "In the 1970s, I raced the Merc a little with the flathead. My friend Reed Hall had a flathead Merc and we'd race every year at the NW Cruise-In. He always won. So one year, I secretly swapped in a 454 big-block Chevy. The big race came and I redlit. I was bummed. Three years later, I learned that Reed had the starter redlight me. It's great to have friends, huh?" Of course, Chuck wants a rematch, now that the '92 is dialed-in. Bring it, Reed! Speaking of racing, is that a Thames, laying in the weeds behind the Merc? (Photo Courtesy Chris Clark) *Right:* The 392 Hemi is 1958 vintage and appears mostly stock. What's going on here, Chuck? "The block is .060 inch over. Has a 4-barrel carb now, but I have a Weiand 3-2 setup with J-2 Olds carbs, for the future. The 2¼-inch exhaust blows through glasspacks. Two adapters—Offy Hemi to early Ford and early Ford to late Ford—hook to the stock clutch lever. I fabbed the engine and trans mounts, using stock Merc rubber biscuits. Stock radiator, water pump, fuel pump, starter, oil filter, and pulleys. Dodge truck flywheel, clutch, and pressure plate. Exhaust manifolds are Chrysler 300 four-bolt. One challenge was making the column shift work: Moved engine forward, modified levers, and built shift rods. Stock Merc Dana 44 rear has 3.91:1 gears and Power-Lok from IHC with 30-spline axles. Bulletproof!" (Photo Courtesy Chris Clark)

5:03 pm, Pacific Standard Time: Steve's Auto Restorations owner Steve Frisbie and crew gather to watch Chuck head home for dinner. This is a daily ritual. It doesn't take him all day to leave the parking lot—Chuck hates cold food. (Photo Courtesy Chris Clark)

The only transmission that fit my needs is a **Borg Warner T-85** with an R-11 overdrive.

Left: Party central is comfy, functional, and unpretentious. Stock accoutrements make squinting through V-butted windshield a time-travel exercise, with deco 1950 peripherals. OEM column shift, steering wheel, and throttle pedal are well worn. Chuck stitched up his own door panels and carpet, years ago. Mega hours in garnish moldings pay off with perfect fit. Stewart Warner temp gauge is throwback to flathead days. Dash is stock, except for poor-man's radio delete. Chuck is considering a Lincoln dash now. (Photo Courtesy Chris Clark) *Right:* Any chopped Merc has an inherent nastiness about it. Add a Hemi for extra pressure on the stock front suspension for a threatening stance. Three-inch rear blocks and skirts keep altitude adjusted. Cover with flat black for evil points, then torch it with green and yellow flames, laid out by Mitch Kim and sprayed by Carl McClanahan. Add pinstripes by Kim and now you have a package to make any daughter's father cringe. Wide whites on red steelies leave no doubt: This is Trouble, with a capitol "T." (Photo Courtesy Chris Clark)

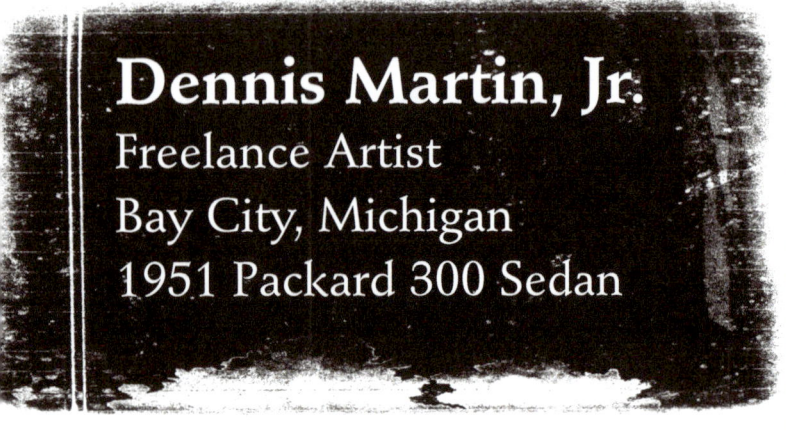

Dennis Martin, Jr.
Freelance Artist
Bay City, Michigan
1951 Packard 300 Sedan

Dennis is a pretty positive guy, but can't help seeing the negative space around a car. That's what artists are trained to do and Dennis has been in training since learning to hold a pencil. Shortly after that, Dennis, Sr. taught him to hold a wrench and destiny took over.

Dennis helped his dad build several muscle cars, accumulating skills for his own future rides. He stumbled across his first Packard early on and has been powerless against their magnetism ever since. Numerous false starts eventually led to this former four-door, bought from pinstriper "Tubs" Welch. By then, Dennis had plenty of Packard parts to use for this project. He'd also been scratching out concept designs for the Damaged Goods shop, so it was natural to team up with them to create this evil custom Tudor. The sedan came with a rebuilt drivetrain and period diamond-tuck interior, but Dennis was seeing negative, regarding the tall top and extra doors. At that point, the torch was lit.

The Damaged Goods crew (Troy Wascher, Mike Bermudez, and Carl Payne) had just finished a similar conversion on Troy's own '51 Packard and agreed to keep the momentum going with Dennis' project. "In no time, my Packard had a two-door conversion using parts from my other Packards, a chopped top using the rear window from Troy's Packard, and lowering blocks on the rear. I took it home and cleaned up the metal work, then it was back to Damaged Goods to get the glass cut and installed by Carl and have Mike reshoot it in red primer. I painted the scallops and my friend Jon 'Lucas' Russell pinstriped them." The effect is distinctly wicked, but it's also a dead-nuts-reliable road dog that devours miles like they're gourmet kibble and does it with the grace of a greyhound.

Dennis says the Packard is definitely a high-smileage car, but adds that there's always room for improvement. "Future plans are mostly to make it more driver friendly, like radials, disc brakes, aluminum radiator, and maybe a TH350 or Torqueflite. I have a factory 4-barrel intake I want to use. I'm also seeing a louvered hood, lake-style pipes, and maybe a different paint job." Dennis' end point: "I'd like to keep just about everything original or vintage, like a time machine. But I also want to drive the hell out of it and that means I need to upgrade. I guess that's what customizing is all about—to make what's out there, better."

"When you start with a car so rusted or damaged that you can hardly give it away, you don't feel bad about chopping it up. It's like giving life to something most people would say is too far gone to bother with." (Photo Courtesy Charlie McCarthy)

Here's all the proof you need of what an artist's vision and craftsman's skills can do to bend any design into their own interpretation. Throw in the motivation of a lifetime passion and you're bound to hit a bullseye, no matter how elusive the target can get at times. Packard's 24th Series design was considered pretty bold in 1951, stodgy by 1960s' standards, and downright quaint after that. One-piece windshield was new for 1951. Terry Kemp caught Dennis lurking around Deer Acres Amusement Park in Pinconning, Michigan, where they don't have a single deer. (Photo Courtesy Terry Kemp)

This is Dennis' official "before" shot. (Photo Courtesy Dennis Martin)

The four-door was solid but **plenty frumpy** when Dennis got it. It had some character, but was still suffering an **identity crisis.**

The epic Packard plant kicked 15,309 of these 300-series sedans out of Detroit in 1951. None looked like this. "It was in great shape, for a Michigan car," says Dennis. He and the Damaged Goods team converted the touring sedan into a two-door and leaned the B-pillars to evoke a fast-back coupe vibe of forward motion. The top was chopped 4½ inches in front and 6½ inches in the rear. The leftover backlight from Troy Wascher's Packard 200 included the wider C-pillar, which was the deal-maker here. Chris Craft speedboat scoops were added to cool engine compartment. The skirts and lowering blocks bring the stance into line with the remaining stock sheet metal, which already sported enough quirky Packard-ness to draw the former family sedan straight into Koolsville. (Photo Courtesy Terry Kemp)

Top: Dennis says, "When I popped the hood and saw this massive straight-8, I thought, 'Sold!'" The 327-ci Packard Thunderbolt boasted 150 hp when new, enough to pull the 3,875-pound sled around with help from the unique Ultramatic trans and 3.52:1 gears. Packard's first year for the oil-bath air cleaner was 1951, but Dennis opted for this sporty scoop on the Carter 2-barrel. A factory 4-barrel setup is standing by for future sprint action. The generator got lost when the 12-volt conversion (via a Painless wiring kit) was performed. (Photo Courtesy Dennis Martin) *Middle:* When Dennis fell for Packards, the art deco interiors were a big part of the attraction. So he left this one alone, but for a smattering of swap meet gauges and a traffic light viewfinder. I think the necker knob fits right in with historic imagery of Packards broadsliding on gravel roads and dirt tracks. You can't see the diamond-tuck seat covers here, but you know Dennis is all over it while working that steering wheel. (Photo Courtesy Terry Kemp) *Bottom:* There are still some rough edges to clean up. Or not. Dennis says, "One thing about rats, you don't worry so much about them. If you get a scratch, you just whip out a can of spray paint and touch it up. If you dent it or something, it just adds character." A little peek at the air box for the hood scoops is shown here. (Photo Courtesy Charlie McCarthy)

Nothing says **Fashion Moderne** like a **Packard grille**

Dennis elected to keep the bumper guards and headlight rings. The shortened side spear completes the brightwork on what was long considered one of America's most garish excesses of plating. Evolving styling perceptions find 1950s Packards at the height of hip today. (Photo Courtesy Terry Kemp)

Definitely a fun shot, but it's all too (painfully) real for some of us. There was a time when the cops wouldn't even attempt to chase down a Hudson or Packard. The officer driving the '58 Dodge Police Special (with a 392-ci Hemi) isn't impressed. Meanwhile, Dennis waits to take his medicine. (Photo Courtesy Terry Kemp)

CHAPTER 2: THE RESURGENCE OF UNFINISHED CARS 59

David and Rebecca Fruits

Industrial Tech Sales and Office Manager
Gardner, Kansas
1953 Chevrolet Coupe

Let's take a short time-out from rabid rat action to savor a sweet love story. Dim the lights, cue Barry White, and turn it down low . . .

We all long to find that special someone to share quiet shop time with, and when David crossed paths with Rebecca, he knew it was almost as momentous as finding his most coveted swap meet score: his beloved '53 Chevy coupe. Why a mid-1950s stovebolt? "This may sound corny, but I saw Jesse James' '54 Chevy and fell in love." So love was in the air from the onset. Knowing that love replaces loss, David didn't flinch when selling his '67 Chevelle to pay for the '53. Things heated up immediately upon committing to the coupe. "I trailered it home and started working on it in my mom's gravel driveway. I swapped in a T-5 and a 1955 rear end, on my back. I lowered it with a cut-off wheel." Some lowering blocks and Posies springs were also involved. Once the stance was declared righteous, disc brakes were added to "lots of homemade parts" and the 235 six-cylinder was tuned up.

That's when David hit the road. "The H.A.M.B. Drags was the maiden voyage. I've been back five times now. Also drove it to the Rust Revival, the Salina [Kansas] KKOA Lead-sled gathering, and to Tulsa, Oklahoma, for Darryl Starbird's show." Jeez, what a great honeymoon—these two were obviously meant to be together. But David also knows that any relationship requires an ongoing effort and commitment, so he's gathered a Jag front suspension, a 350 Chevy/700R-4 combo, a set of air bags, an aluminum fuel cell, and a set of 15-inch-diameter wheels as investments in the happy couple's future.

Oh yeah—on January 19, 2008, David and Rebecca committed, too. These are their wedding photos. They drove the Chevy from Gardner to Kansas City through a good ol' Midwest ice storm to make it happen.

"It was minus 3 degrees and she ran like a champ! The reception was at the same Scottish Temple as the wedding. They used to have the Kansas City Auto Show there, because the elevator was the only one big enough to lift Cadillacs to the stage." Damn, this guy knows romance! And what happened later that night, David? You know, when you finally got to be alone? "We just cruised off into the sunset and never looked back." Oh.

*"I don't give a *%$# how they do it in California!" (Photo Courtesy David Fruits)*

The "Just Married" lettering was still wet, applied only hours before the wedding.

Top Left: Hey, why don't you two go get a room?! You'll fog up the windows! (Photo Courtesy David Fruits) *Top Right:* I think the coupe is plenty happenin' as is, with the six-cylinder/5-speed combo, cut coils, and blocks. But David says by the time you read this, a Jag front clip, 350/700R4, and 15-inch wheels with full covers will be added. I think it'll still look cool in front of the house, and the V-8 will be more appropriate to David's background. His uncles used to run 426 Hemi stock cars at Lakeside Speedway in Kansas City, "back in the day." (Photo Courtesy David Fruits) *Middle Left:* Young love in the parking lot. And Rebecca doesn't even look jealous! (Photo Courtesy David Fruits) *Middle Right:* "Gosh Becky, that was a swell wedding, huh?" "Jeepers, I'll say! And our Chevy is the ginchiest getaway car ever! Step on it, David!" "Hey Dollface, I got my two-tones through the floorboards already!" (Photo Courtesy David Fruits) *Bottom:* Buzzing away into the sunset never looked so warm and fuzzy, no matter the frigid temps. Good luck, you crazy kids! (Photo Courtesy David Fruits)

Nick Kout
Fabrication Shop Supervisor
Colorado Springs, Colorado
1953 Pontiac Two-door Hardtop

Some projects fall together effortlessly, with an air of divine intervention about them. Some begin with best intentions, but shrivel up and die of neglect. The successful ones often involve a key third party, usually a family member. This Pontiac's tale includes all of the above elements and there's even a deceptive twist at the end. Juicy . . .

Nick's a pro by day and hobbyist at night. The nocturnal builds of his '40 Ford coupe and '68 Mustang were major successes, thanks to help from father-in-law Gene Musick (who's been rodding since the 1950s). Gene scored this Pontiac in 1985. Nick was there. "He promptly installed a Nova subframe, then disassembled the front clip and sandblasted the sheet metal in preparation for a slick paint job. Then the project stalled, while he helped me build my '40 coupe. Fast forward 20 years and the old Poncho is still sitting. At that point, I convinced Gene to let me finish the car 'as is' and make it a driver. He agreed and the result is what you see here." Good result, Nick! Here's how he got it:

Nick rebuilt the Nova stub, adding disc brakes while he was at it. He stabbed in a 350/350 he was tired of tripping over. A Maverick rear end was deemed a good fit and installed. A spare 1968 Mustang gas tank fit right in, too. After a re-wire, the key was twisted and "Job done; it's a driver!" Nick hit the road and hit it hard, getting positive feedback with every mile under the whitewalls. "So I decided to go ahead and finish the paint. I called on Wayne Saunders at Alternative Automotive Design in Colorado Springs, who specializes in custom paint and woodgraining. Wayne said, 'No problem! Let's just repaint the front clip in the stock green,' then he re-created the wear and rust to the point that no one even notices!"

The coupe and Mustang were assigned standby status when the Pontiac became the ride du jour. "This has quickly become my favorite car to drive and I owe it all to my father-in-law Gene. My wife Kelley and I have driven it over 10,000 miles in the last couple years. I love it when people ask when we're gonna paint it and I say, 'We *did* paint it.' They just look at us like we've hit our heads."

"I think we've gotten away from making things simple. Since finishing this car, I've realized this is what cars were all about. It's fine wherever it's parked and gets more attention than the shiny stuff. That's drawn me back to the roots of old car building. I'm currently putting together a '40 Ford sedan that's been parked indoors since 1956."

Town and country
—the tin Indian makes both scenes on a regular basis.

Fun doesn't discriminate based on geography and the Pontiac fits in anywhere.

"I've been into cars since high school; worked as a service manager at a few dealerships and even did a stint as a street rod shop owner in the 1990s. I have a few shiny cars, too nice to drive. You worry about parking, paint chips, etc. What fun is that?"

Wife Kelley loves the '53 and is *fiercely protective* of it.

"She loved this car when everyone else thought it was ugly. Now, when we're at a show and everyone wants to buy it, she's the first to say, 'No way! It's never for sale!'" Oh yeah? Then why'd she let you park it right under that giant boulder about to fall? Who's name is on the insurance?

Top Left: Interior is mostly original, but does have fresh threads on the seats, floor, and headliner. Why mess with 1953 chic? Big fun, from the factory. A tilt Caddy column (and shifter) support original 1953 wheel. Nick installed an EZ Wiring kit to kick-start the original gauges and switches. *Top Right:* Nick confides, "I happened to have a 350 Chevy and TH350 transmission laying around," and they bolted into the Nova stub in minutes. Sorry Poncho purists, but this drivetrain was irresistible. Cast scoop hides Edelbrock carb and manifold on otherwise dead-stock mill. Reliability reigns here. A 3.08:1, 1974 Maverick 8-inch Ford brings up the rear. The perfect freeway flier combo.

Top: In the Alternative Automotive Design paint booth, just after Wayne Saunders matched front clip finish to rest of car. Fake patina has definitely evolved into an art style of its own! And like all art, it's controversial. *Bottom Left:* The Kout kids have moved on, but, "This summer, grandson Brennan will be ready to ride." So that's four generations to experience the Pontiac rat happenings. And it's all Gene Musick's fault! Left to right: Ryan, Nick, Brennan, Kelley, and Gene lean on the Pontiac in more ways than one. *Bottom Right:* Brennan drives the Kout's heritage straight into the future. Hey! Eyes on the road, man!

CHAPTER 2: THE RESURGENCE OF UNFINISHED CARS

Troy Wascher and Mike Bermudez
Chassis Fabricators
Bay City, Michigan
1957 Pontiac Two-door Hardtop and 1939 Ford Pickup

What's going on here?! Grinders, hammers, and laughter echo through the neighborhood with funhouse surrealism. Then, the song of a full-throated V-8 screams through the din and you know this must be the Damaged Goods shop. Troy Wascher, Mike Bermudez, and Carl Payne supply the frantic thrash soundtrack all day via customer cars and jam on their own creations at night. I chose two of Damaged Goods' personal cars as examples of what the noise is all about.

Troy's Pontiac was found "languishing in a friend's backyard, disassembled and on blocks. I knew as soon as I saw the patina, I had to have it." Two years of haggling later, he had it. Step One was an altitude adjustment via air bag suspension, while leaving the body "as found" (turns out, the patina was only skin deep). The bagged stance was an improvement, "but not low enough, so lower front control arms were fabricated, as well as a monster notch and four-link in the rear. Still not low enough! The decision was made to channel the huge body over the frame, for that rocker-laying look." Mission accomplished.

A genuine tin Indian drivetrain was swapped in from a Trans Am and Troy was in business, driving his point home every night. Troy reports that it runs hard, drives great, and the attention it steals away from more upscale rides is icing on the cake.

Mike pieced his truck together old-school, but got the same results as Troy. He found a 1939 Ford 1½-ton cab and a (1970s) International Scout and started there. The Damaged Goods boys gave the cab their standard "Diablo Chop," establishing some proportions to work from. The Scout frame was turned around backward and narrowed 8 inches in the (new) front. A 1948 Ford front suspension was hung from quarter-elliptic leaves and an 8-inch Ford rear end was attached with tiny parallel leaves from a Cushman three-wheeled cart. Mike tossed in a 403 Olds and a TH350 to handle the big-rig torque and added a downsized 1940s Chevy bed, so it'd still resemble a truck. Now, hammered and slammed and wearing 20-inch-diamater rear wheels and 17-inch front runners, the truck sports a most aggressive demeanor, while remaining somehow accessible and identifiable to the average bear. And Mike is working the wheel, every chance he gets.

Yeah, the Damaged Goods guys are noisy neighbors. But nobody in the industrial zone is complaining much and the customers are all satisfied. The music mostly serenades the Saginaw Bay and dissipates over Lake Huron. No damage done. Good.

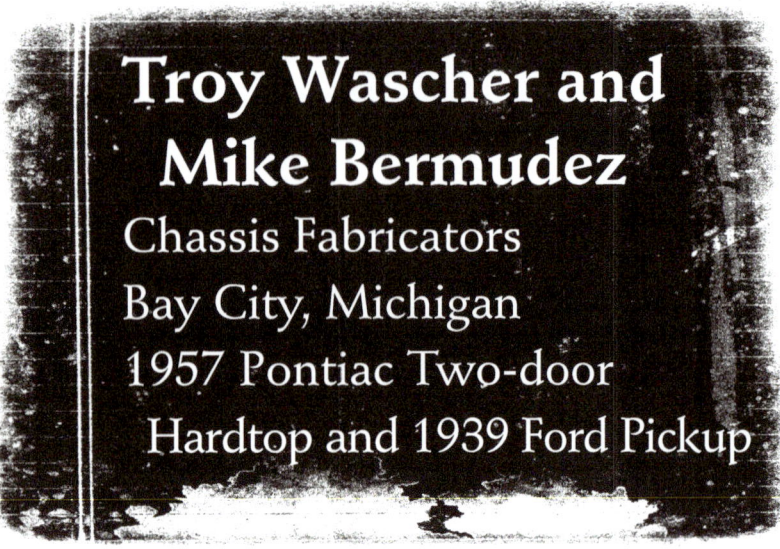

"We have a great deal of **passion** toward the hobby and each of us has our own **talents, taste, and vision** that we try to incorporate **into each build.**"

A 400-inch 1978 Trans Am engine with mild cam, 650-cfm 4-barrel on Edelbrock intake, and 2½-inch exhaust blowing through Flowmasters help plant the nose in the dirt. The TH-400 transmission came with the engine. The coveted 1957 Poncho (3.08:1) rear end is still in there, deeming the Troy toy a frequent freeway flier. Those wheels are '64 Buick Rivieras, with blasted and painted centers. They work well on the '57 and get OEM bonus points. Mike's truck sneaks into the picture at this point. (Photos Courtesy Silas Warren)

Above: Troy's Chieftain looks right at home, lurking in the sinister shade of a surreal landscape. Setting the mood are 2,600-pound air bags all around with four-way independent control, custom A-arms (front), four-link (rear), substantial frame notches, and 3 inches of channeling. He says, "It rides nice!" You also get a peek at the welded-chain steering wheel (there's a matching shift lever inside). (Photo Courtesy Silas Warren) *Below:* This manic Buck Rogers vision of a lunar explorer is just Mike Bermudez's jigsaw puzzle hot rod. The cab, grille, and hood sides all came from the 1½-ton truck he started with, but have been scaled down with plenty of cuts, welds, and geometry equations. (Photo Courtesy Silas Warren)

Above: Under the arching hood lies 403 inches of Oldsmopower, backed by a TH350 transmission. The rear end is 3.42:1-geared 8-inch Ford, pirated from a '73 Mustang and narrowed to fit. Mike is plenty happy with the insane torque-to-weight ratio, as the gearing makes for hellacious sprints (when he can get traction). The seats and steering box are from the same victimized International Scout that was robbed of its frame. (Photo Courtesy Silas Warren) Below: If you spy this pair out on the road and you can keep up, follow 'em back to the Damaged Goods shop—playground of manic mechanics and birthplace of whimsically feral rods and customs. Just check your ego at the door. (Photo Courtesy Silas Warren)

CHAPTER 2: THE RESURGENCE OF UNFINISHED CARS

Chapter 3

THE TREND CATCHES FIRE
—RESPECTABLE RATS?

Lane Leipold's '40 Ford pickup. (Photo Courtesy Scott Parkhurst)

GOING MAINSTREAM AT FULL-VOLUME SWAGGER

The pendulum eventually found its way back to center. So centered that the mainstream caught wind and we saw the further commercialization of hot rodding, via the rat rods! Who'da thunk it. But it happened.

"The look" was interpreted by everyone from Hollywood scenesters to clothing marketeers, and the cars became mere fashion accessories. Bizarre. The good news is, many people were exposed to the car scene for the first time and a new generation took special notice—kids love rat rods!

These rolling cartoons captured the fancy of a generation of future knuckle busters and the result is already impacting America's streets. Skulls, spikes, and spiderwebs are popping up on Hondas, 4x4s, and jet skis. Rockabilly music has enjoyed a resurgence that now finds it drifting out of PT Cruiser windows. Everyone including the family dog has a tattoo now. The rats have definitely left a mark. But they haven't left the building. In fact, if you want to see ingenuity on wheels and find whatever happened to America's sense of humor, you need look no farther than your nearest rat's nest.

And so we present a brief look at the mainstreaming of outlaw hot rodding. The ultimate oxymoron, or the opening of the floodgates? Yes. These are real-life people, enjoying the fruits of rats in the real world. They bring a fresh enthusiasm to the salad, which is always good for any party.

This "fresh blood" transfusion is perfectly natural. The average bear on the street, who hasn't invested decades of research into following rodding's evolving nuances, doesn't know what to make of cars that induce drooling in others. But they can see what a rat is all about at a glance. Likewise, the timing is perfect for aspiring hot rod and muscle car builder/owners, intimidated at the prospect of a lengthy and expensive project. Rats are a seductive alternative with a fun factor that makes them all the more attractive. Just like the rat bikes before them, rat rods are decidedly sexy on many levels. The public got that message loud and clear. Today, rats are considered the people's toys.

Mike Butler's '30 Ford Tudor.
(Photo Courtesy Rory Bright)

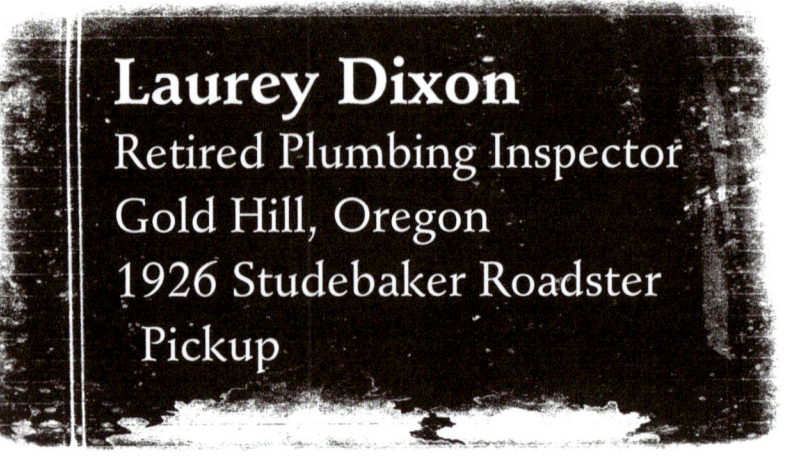

Laurey Dixon
Retired Plumbing Inspector
Gold Hill, Oregon
1926 Studebaker Roadster Pickup

e're seeing more of this lately: Builders score orphan tin on the cheap, hatch a plan for a unique rat, mock it up, then tear it back down and become obsessed with straightening sheet metal and grinding welds. They just can't help themselves. The result is a nicely finished car with rat personality intact. Someone will coin a snappy name for these well dressed rats soon enough. I'll just call 'em "dressers" for now.

Laurey lives the good (retired) life in "God's Country," with wife Gayle, son Bret, and best friend Norton (the basset hound). A somewhat eccentric rodder, he's known locally for his '50 Chevy hot rod ambulance. But the ambulance was excluded from the pre-1948 clique and Laurey wanted in. He sold a parcel of real estate to finance a turnkey ride, the most cost efficient way to go rodding. But once on the hunt, Laurey realized that any car he bought would always be known as the builder's car, not his own. Fortunately, Laurey enjoys getting his hands dirty and decided to build his own.

A visit to local vintage tin hoarder Sherman Parker resulted in a bargain Studebaker touring car body and an offer to help build it. The body was cut down to its essence and Sherm fabbed a pickup bed and a nosepiece. A sturdy 2x3-inch frame was created, kicked up front and rear for appropriate stance and center of gravity. The standard early Ford front suspension was embellished with Custom Metal center-pivot friction shocks and a four-bar/buggy-spring hybrid system at the rear.

Laurey is known as the local mag wheel fetishist, and vintage magnesium Americans keep his legend rolling. The custom and hot rod elements created a snarky silhouette with a cool stance. But Laurey found the quilt-work body panels distracting and before he realized it, the entire truck was rubbed smooth and covered in paint (albeit via Krylon spray cans).

Now Laurey finds himself in hot rod purgatory, as bystanders struggle to categorize the car, too ratty for traditionalists and too anal for Ratburg. He's been refused entry to some shows and kicked out of others. But Laurey built it to drive. He and Norton have put over 4,000 miles a year on the rude Stude since the Nailhead was broken in, back in 2003. They look sharp, blasting past car shows and rolling down the road to somewhere. Maybe someday, categorical labeling will become passé. Until then, Laurey can only hope to hear someone say, "Cool Dresser, man." For now, he's a true outcast.

"I had so much fun building my rat rod! But when it was done, people said, 'That's not a rat rod.' The terminology was more important to them than the car itself! What the — ?!"

I spent some quality time bombing around Gold Hill (Pop: 1,080) with Laurey and Norton. Encircled by the Rogue River, bridges at each end of town allow access, the epitome of small town America. Bud Crayne would fit right in here.

The truck ran and drove great, inducing whiplash wherever we went.

It's actually a 1923 (or 1924) body, but Laurey licensed it as a 1926, because that's the title he had. Sherm Parker shortened and deepened a 1933 Ford truck grille to make the nosepiece, fabbed the steel bed from scratch, hammer formed the tailgate, and molded it all together. Sherm also re-curved the aluminum T roadster windshield frame, welded up by Royal Kenton. Satin-black and turquoise Krylon Norton-proof all of the sweaty labor, on display here at Del Rio Vineyards (preferred luncheon spot of indigenous cosmopolitan rodents).

The front suspension employs early Ford components mixed with Fake Jakes' disc brake covers and a Flaming Industries Vega steering box. Jamie Ford at Custom Metal supplied the center-pivot friction shocks. The road grader headlights use vintage aftermarket lenses. This combination drives Norton wild.

Laurey says, "Hey, when you're sitting in here all day, it better be stylish and comfy!" It is. Royal Kenton made the seat and door panels, then covered them with leather. The Stewart Warner gauges ride in 1932 Chevy insert. The Gennie Shifter with baseball knob was bent to clear Stude dash. The Schroeder four-spoke Sprint Car wheel (with pad) tops stainless column by Parker. Door handles are by Chicago Faucet (hot and cold).

Rear suspension is based on Parker-fabbed four-bars and transverse leaf. Plenty of details to ponder at stoplights, like the Laurey-crafted Studebaker script and fun bracketry by Sherm.

Beyond the Model T fuel tank (striped by Turk, a plumber from Riverside, California, who did all lines on truck), Norton is getting antsy to hit the road. Laurey hopped in, hit the GO button, and that's just what they did.

CHAPTER 3: THE TREND CATCHES FIRE

Mike Butler
Retired Motor Home Manufacturer
Chicago Park, California
1930 Ford Tudor

"If Stroker McGurk drove a sedan, this would be it," was Mike's impression when he first saw this Tudor at a show in Idaho. And he couldn't get it out of his head. Six months of haggling later, it took up residence in his garage. Mike lists the slant chop and W-head engine as selling points, but the biggie was that the original builder was 6 feet tall. This was good news for 6 foot-plus Mike, since they don't sell rat rods at the Big & Tall store. He still had to lower the seats, but now reports that the car fits him "perfectly."

The real kicker was how the "Power Plus Special" makes no bones about wearing its ratatude on its sleeve. Yeah, it's cleaner than most, but is still obviously a rat at first sight. Mike's been in the hot rod scene long enough not to care what people think of it. It's his car and that's all that matters to him.

Originally built by Rob Steusloff in Post Falls, Idaho (which is really quite a happenin' hot rod town), the foundation is a 2x4-inch tube frame, kicked up 16 inches in the rear. De rigueur early Ford suicide front suspension hangs on bent wishbones and quarter-elliptic springs. Coil-overs support a 9-inch Ford rear. The top was chopped 5 inches in front and is stock height in the rear. A 1959 348-ci W-block was carefully rebuilt to OEM specs, with a TH350 for backup.

Once in his possession, Mike "roofed it, for those hot days in the sun," noting that "It's more of a springtime rod, as there are no windows." He also added more baffles to the header collectors, as "the noise was something else!" And he does actually drive it. The sedan has been driven a lot more than worked on since Mike first took ownership more than three years ago. He whipped it like a mule to southern California and back, "otherwise, a lot of so-called 'short trips,'" Mike says with a wink, adding, "It's a blast to drive and handles very good."

Mike Butler earned his way into power plus status the hard way. His first job was screwing travel trailers together on the assembly line and he did it until retiring from the same industry, decades later. That's a lot of time to consider how to spend retirement. Time well spent, I'd say.

"No comment."
(Photo Courtesy Rory Bright)

The wedge chop (2 inches in back, 4 inches up front) really drives home the raked stance. Mike says he can see out of it just fine. The Deuce shell was whacked 4 inches, too. The rear panel is well ventilated and bullet holes are for real (don't ask). (Photos Courtesy Rory Bright, top; Dave Taylor, middle and left)

Nothin' like a W-head mill to make a muscular statement. The '59 348 is a "mild build" that still smokes the Cokers with a tickle of the throttle. A lowrider alternator, re-pop Caddy air cleaner, and cowl-mounted steering are tasty touches. TH350 and 3.25:1 gear in a 9-inch Ford rear have eaten everything the 348 has dished out, so far. (Photo Courtesy Rory Bright, left; Dave Taylor, right)

Atmosphere is an inside job. The upholstered bomber seating, Stewart Warner gauges, Sprint Car wheel, and gunnysack door panels set the stage for asphalt hijinx. Large handle at driver's door actuates manual semaphore. (Photo Courtesy Dave Taylor)

It rides smooth and sweet as syrup, thanks to 1946 front axle with Speedway disc brakes on bent 'bones, quarter-elliptic front springs, and coil-overs in back. Lever-action shocks still get the job done on tired twenty-first-century roads. The Power Plus special chews up mega miles with Mike's club, the Roadents. (Photo Courtesy Rory Bright)

Mike, going **nowhere fast.** It's what he does...

Lane Leipold
Pre-sentence Investigator
Lakeville, Minnesota
1940 Ford Pickup

hile rats are generally home-built, we're seeing a shift now, as builders sell off the last project to finance the next one. Lane got his from builders Brian and Richard Thomas (and their associate, James Lavery) in Salt Lake City, Utah. Originally painted olive drab and owned by Uncle Sam, the truck kept pretty busy during World War II, then saw extended duty as a Mountain Bell Telephone rig. Team Thomas acquired it in 2006 and spent a year on the build.

Lane got wind of the project and flew to Salt Lake in late November 2007, where he picked up the truck and left that same night for Minnesota, 1,600 miles away ("No windows, heater, mufflers, or radio at that time"). The drive was a high-velocity funfest and Lane hasn't slowed down yet. "The workmanship on this truck is confirmed by the more than 20,000 problem-free miles I've put on her." As a bonus, when Lane crossed paths with Brian, Richard, and James, a bond was forged. "I've come to call these guys my friends. All three are terrifically talented people—true hot rodders and fabricators." That kind of customer feedback can only be earned with plenty of honesty and sweat.

Built on a 1939 Ford coupe frame, the foundation supports 1941 Ford truck front suspension and a leaf-spring/ladder-bar combo out back, holding a brute-strength Dana 60. A tri-power 406-ci small-block Chevy and TH350 transmission probably makes for a peppy combo in the 2,500-pound trucklet, eh, Lane? "My wife Wendy refuses to ride in it—it absolutely hauls ass! I recently beat a 96-ci Harley in a quarter-mile race." Dang! And does that buggy-sprung chassis provide a nice, firm ride? "I describe the ride quality as being very similar to what a large workbench would have." Got it.

By following his intuition to the right people, Lane was able to climb in, turn the key, and drive away in a mean-ass truck that scares his wife silly, gives his daughter Angelyn the giggles (she rides shotgun to Bonneville and back every year), and is more reliable than the family dog. He's beyond satisfied. Maybe adopting a homeless rat from a quality breeder is the short path to long laughs? Lane Leipold sure makes it look appealing.

"Been to a car show lately? The rats attract a lot of interest. I love some of them and wouldn't be caught dead in others. I fear some P.O.S. deathtrap rat will crash and kill someone and the government pain-in-the-asses will pass a bunch of new laws and screw it up for all of us." (Photo Courtesy Scott Parkhurst)

The tire smoke machine—a 1972 406-inch small-block runs triple Stromberg 97s on an Edelbrock manifold. The ported OEM heads use roller rockers on pinned studs. All that fuel is easily ignited by a Joe Hunt magneto. Cam is your basic Isky hydraulic RV gruntmaster. Gases are blown out by Thomas headers. It's a relatively mild combo that's very streetable, but blasts out gobs of grin-inducing torque. A TH350 and Dana 60 take the brunt of the grunt. The "#1 High Horse" lettering on block must be secret racer code for something (his other ride is a '56 Chevy drag car; Lane's a lifelong racer). Note the plug wires and hard lines. Fun and tasty. (Photos Courtesy Scott Parkhurst)

The vibe here is definitely back-alley street race chic!

Don't let the 1936 truck grille trip you up. The cab is a 1940, so that's what's listed on the title. The 1940 hood was tweaked to fit. The Thomas boys shortened a Deuce bed 22 inches and whacked the top of the cab 7½ inches while they were at it. A kicked and partially boxed 1939 frame is now strong enough to support the Moon tank. The early Ford front suspension (right down to the Houdaille shocks) looks sharp, dressed with ET III 10-spokes. Out back, ladder bars locate a leaf-sprung Dana 60 rear with 3.54:1 gears. Custom steelies by Rally America Wheels spin grooved Hurst slicks. (Photo Courtesy Scott Parkhurst)

The cartoonie sky-high shifter is **visually fun,** but could be a **knuckle scraper!**

Facing Page: Sit down, strap in, and enjoy a blurred view of America through the chopped 1940 windshield. The original 1940 commercial dash (with auxiliary Stewart-Warner gauges) and a 1938 wheel set the tone inside. Headliner is made from a U.S. Army tent. Note the spotlight handle (I don't want to know what the spotlight gets used for). Lane's 15-year-old daughter, Angelyn, is his main shotgun rider, so World War II belts are employed on the vinyl-covered bench seat (showing signs of puckering). (Photo Courtesy Scott Parkhurst) *Top:* Besides filthy car parts, tools, and beer coolers, the hacked Deuce bed also totes the main fuel tank. The trailer hitch is reminder of truck's utilitarian nature. The pinstriping is by Sinclair and continues under truck. (Photo Courtesy Scott Parkhurst) *Bottom:* Tailgaters can enjoy the sand-cast Dana 60 cover by Brian Thomas, while challengers usually get a fleeting glimpse of Lane's taillight collection. (Photo Courtesy Scott Parkhurst)

CHAPTER 3: THE TREND CATCHES FIRE 83

Chad Sinnen
Service Tech
Shakopee, Minnesota
1946 Ford Pickup

Chad wears the crusty grime under his fingernails proudly, because it got there honestly. His dad and uncle Jon were both influences, exposing him to mechanical shenanigans from day one. By age 13, Chad had scored a Galaxy 500 on the sly, making clandestine test drives and stashing it a few blocks from home. When the police inevitably arrived to investigate the neighbor's complaints of screaming engines and smoking tires, the jig was up. "I got in some trouble and so did the older kid who sold me the car."

Not long after the Galaxy experience, a gas station job financed a '70 Chevelle build ("I wish I still had that one!") and Chad's course was set. But an incident at the Sturgis bike run made an impact that would knock Chad a bit off course.

"An old beater Panhead was sitting by a bunch of high-dollar bikes, but everybody was standing around the Panhead. That's when I started getting into the rat look."

Chad was building a '34 truck when he chanced upon this '46 on Craigslist.org. He chased it over a couple years of near misses, but finally tracked it down and snapped it up. It was a driver, so the poor old '34 never got touched again (and was soon sold), as Chad quickly piled up the miles on the '46 and slowly tweaked it to his liking. As of this writing, Chad has put more than 10,000 miles on the odometer, providing him and the family with about 10,000 adventures.

Here is a small sample of my favorites: entering a flame-throwing contest and starting the driver's-side door paint on fire(!); entering a local burnout contest, where the '46 came out with the flamethrowers blazing and proceeded to do donuts for a good five minutes, before being excused. "The whitewalls were a little worse for wear, but I had a lot of fun." Oh yeah, there was the stoplight three-way, with a Trailblazer SS *and* a Nissan 300ZX: "The old rat took both of those built-up rides for the first two-and-a-half blocks. The thing actually goes pretty good." A couple of books could be filled with the entire collection, but you get the picture. Chad's longtime sweetheart, Deb, almost always joins in the fun, along with her daughter Emmy and son Alex, who's harder to remove from the cab than 90-weight fumes—he's probably in there right now!

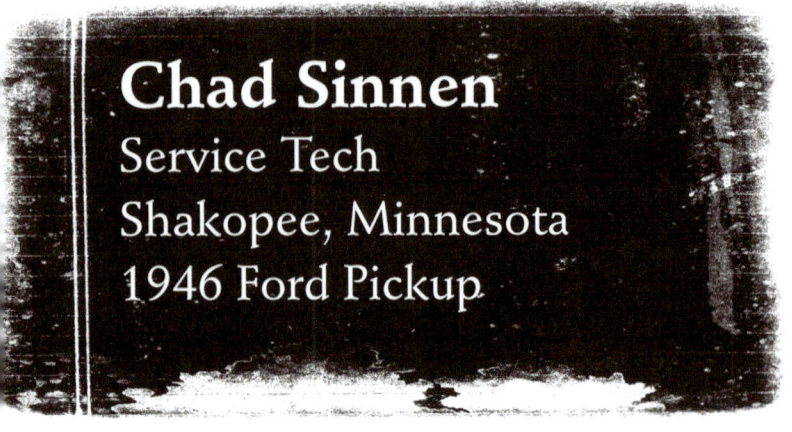

"I think the rat rods are going to keep getting cooler and more popular, with new rides taking it further and further. The future looks good." (Photo Courtesy Scott Parkhurst)

The 1946 cab was chopped 4½ inches and channeled 5 inches. It sits on a 1937 frame, shortened 8 inches. Front suspension features a 5-inch-drop M.A.S. axle, 1942 Ford brakes, Vega steering box, Monroe shocks, and Speedway hairpins. The rear suspension is a triangulated four-link with QA1 coil-overs. Wide whitewall Firestones on 1935 Ford wires make the rolling beauty statement, while 1934 caps offer up some bling. (Photo Courtesy Scott Parkhurst)

The pinstriped rhino horn (previously a garbage truck exhaust stack) directs oxygen to a Weber carb on the Chevy 350. The 4-barrel, HEI, and headers help the small-block produce respectable snort. A Turbo 350 trans with a 2600 stall converter sends the juice to a 3.08:1 posi Camaro rear. White firewall is a fun, traditional touch, setting off the engine nicely. Shortly after these pictures were shot, Chad added injected flamethrowers to the Speedway header collectors. I've seen them in action and the flames are scary huge! (Photo Courtesy Scott Parkhurst)

The Crank'M Out Customs graphics promote original builder Jason Pohl's shop. Chad's fine with giving Jason some free ink here. Park Chad's truck next to a stock '46 and you'd never guess they're the same year, thanks to open wheels and the 1936 truck grille, completely changing the aesthetic from farm truck to hoodlum hauler! (Photo Courtesy Scott Parkhurst)

The 1937 Ford box was shortened 13 inches. It's still big enough to cover the rear kickup and suspension, while hauling cold Miller (actually, the battery rides in the cooler). It also gave Chad something to bolt the early Ford taillights to. (Photo Courtesy Scott Parkhurst)

Hey Chad, can I live in your shop?

Serapes never go out of style (neither do tiny sombreros). The '53 Dodge insert in a 1946 dash now sports electric gauges. Steering wheel is also from a '53 Mopar. The Moon tachometer supplies bonus info. The Lokar shifter gives Chad total control of torque band without crawling under truck with Vice Grips. Wiring throughout truck is by Haywire. (Photo Courtesy Scott Parkhurst)

Kristin Martin
Teacher/Waitress/Photojournalist
Los Angeles, California
1955 Studebaker Champion

Little known fact: Rat bites never heal. Luckily, Kristin Martin got a ferocious infection, although it appeared innocuous at first. "Ever since getting into vintage fashion as a teenager, I wanted a vintage car to complete the look. Being of the mindset that you shouldn't drive a classic car unless you can work on it, I started asking some mechanical questions, such as, "How does an engine work, Grandpa?" Kristin spent 10 years studying the habits of the North American hot rod before trying one on for size.

"When I finally decided to buy a classic car of my own, my daily driver, I was on a limited budget and thought I'd go for something simple and common, like a Ford Falcon." But Kristin was raised in a Studebaker family. Sooo . . . "When I found the listing for a '55 Stude coupe in the newspaper, I knew I needed to go look at it. It was love at first sight! I can't imagine not taking 'Studie' home with me that day."

Now bitten and smitten, Kristin committed, big time. "My best friend let me share her car for the year and a half it took me to get Studie on the road." Already updated with a Stude V-8, that engine was pronounced DOA and Kristin's genetic Studebaker allegiance pragmatically went south. The carless teacher took on a waitressing side-job to finance a small-block Chevy instead and soon snagged a stroked version (with transmission) from someone's abandoned hot rod Studebaker project (pure kismet). Being garageless too, a local shop did the swap while Kristin reupholstered the interior. "After many months and many waitressing tips, I was done. I picked Studie up and hours later, ventured out across the Mojave Desert by myself to attend Viva Las Vegas. I didn't have any issues during the trip!"

It only got worse after that. "Now I get my hands dirty whenever something comes up. From changing a transmission, rebuilding the suspension, and overhauling my brakes; there's been too many adventures to record! Meeting up with other wrenchin' ladies and forming my club, the Gasoline Girls, has been fun. Learning how to do burnouts at Gene Winfield's house [after attending his metal-working course] and driving to Bonneville for Speedweek in the middle of the night to avoid daytime heat and meeting [the] racing Studebakers out there was a blast!" Kristin prays the bite never heals. "I don't plan on making many changes to this car and am not sure if I'll ever do the bodywork and paint on it . . . she's too perfect the way she is."

For more Kristin and Studie action, www.GreaseGirl.com, www.MyRideisMe.com, and www.GasolineGirls.com have the fix.

"It doesn't take guys long to realize I'm into the mechanics of my car. I've got grease under my nails and in my skin, just like them. My dream is to one day open a garage of my own. The low-dollar budget of the rat rods and the intrinsic creativity of the style have attracted a whole new face to the [hot rod] hobby." (Photo Courtesy Kristin Martin)

Sorry Steadybreaker dudes, Kristin's rude Stude gets its 'tude from a 383-ci, snot flingin', mystery small-block. "It was built by whoever owned the car it came from, so I don't have all the specs." It's torquey, but sings too, thanks to a peaky, solid flat-tappet cam and roller rockers. A Holley 4150 on a Weiand Team G single-plane manifold feeds it and custom headers and exhaust system by Kristin and B&C Industries expel the waste. Kristin swapped in the 700R4 after killing the previous three trannies with "enthusiastic" driving. The 700 is holding steady, and the 3.55:1-geared 9-inch Ford has also proven to be bulletproof. Kristin coyly understates, "She's fast. I love that it's always got extra power when I need it." (Photo Courtesy Kristin Martin)

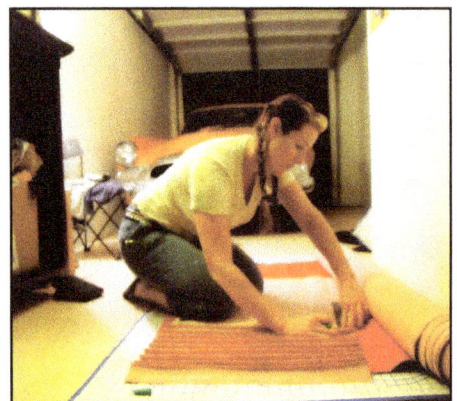

Top: This is bucks-down rodding, personified. It's her only car and is coin operated, via waitressing tips. Kristin added ABS brakes while rebuilding the stock suspension and steering. "I'm very confident, driving in L.A. traffic. I do it every day, speeding down the freeway at 80 mph." (Photo Courtesy Kristin Martin) *Bottom Left:* Kristin is one of the proud few to have stitched up their own interior. A retro Hawaiian barkcloth was used, along with glitter vinyl for the headliner and package tray. It came out pretty snarky! (Photo Courtesy Kristin Martin) *Bottom Midde and Right:* Flaking the top was a typical Gasoline Girls club project. Everyone had a blast learning and the results are ooh la la!, forever. (Photos Courtesy Kristin Martin)

Top Left to Right: A day in the life—after a morning thrash, Kristin heads out for a test drive/parts run, changes into some evening wear for socializing purposes, then finally gives Studie a well-deserved rest. Kristin disclosed no details on events after sundown. (Photos Courtesy Kristin Martin) *Bottom:* Full Moons are the defining characteristic, spreading the salty Studie gospel from Bonneville to all points east, west, north, and south. (Photo Courtesy Kristin Martin)

Yeah, that's the original paint.

CHAPTER 3: THE TREND CATCHES FIRE   91

Chapter 4

A NEW BREED OF EXTREME RODS
—XXX HARDCORE BARE METAL PHOTOS!

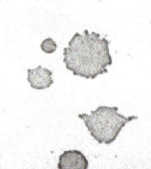

Dylan Patterson's 1929 Ford Tudor. (Photo Courtesy Scott Parkhurst)

YOU MUST BE 18 TO VIEW THIS CHAPTER

This is the backlash to the backlash. The point here is that rats are more than a trend. The attitude seems to be, "If you're not hardcore, you're just a poser." Got to separate 'em. Fine.

This is the natural order of the sociopolitical structure—everything comes around to this, eventually. Conversely, every generation strives to brand its discoveries as its own—in the process, losing details that fall out and roll to the shoulder of the road, nevermore to make sense of the puzzle it once fit into. So it is with rat rods. Gen X sprinkled Pabst Blue Ribbon, psychobilly, and skatepunk/race-car-style graphics into the recipe that began as Camels, jazz, and primer. But since change *is* the natural order, it all seems—well—natural.

As a niche within a niche, ratdom opens itself to the same propensity for obsession as any other attraction to the lunatic fringe. From the initial attraction and inspiration to the build process and the consequent rat patrolling from scene to scene, there are many opportunities to dive head-first into the deep end of rat infested waters and wallow away. Many people seem to "find" themselves in the fellowship. Others get so lost in the nuts and bolts that they become almost oblivious to any life forms at all.

More irony. Born of the solitary lone wolf ethos, rat rodding now supports many car clubs that wouldn't otherwise exist. These micro-sociopolitical experiments are a refuge for many outcasts who wouldn't normally join any club that would have them as a member. Yet bonds are forged, as well as the occasional pissing match, teaching them valuable human relations lessons. Does that make them any less extreme? All we know is, as rats flirt with the boundaries of acceptability, both the cars and the owners take ever bigger chances. We love them for that. These gambles are rarely seen today in other facets of rodding, where fear of rejection rules the road. Rats laugh at such trepidation. It's the honest, heartfelt release-from-way-down-in-the-soul laugh of someone who's earned it the hard way. The hardcores. The lifers. The new breed of extremists.

Sergey Sadovnik's 1967 Likhachev ZIL-157. (Photo Courtesy Irina Pichugin)

Dennis Bradford
Fabricator
Camas, Washington
1919 Dodge Modified

"Well, this just figures. I mean, I've never had anything but beaters, so nobody was surprised that I'd build this for my first open-wheeled hot rod." So speaketh Dennis Bradford, upon stumbling into this topless joint after decades of looking in from the outside. He enjoyed himself in the meantime, though. "I started washing parts for my grandpa when I was five. He taught me to weld at age nine." Today, Dennis works exclusively on crusty tin, but always aspired to own a fenderless/topless car. "The ultimate hot rods!" declares Dennis. So when he spied a '19 Dodge Touring sitting in a buddy's back yard, you know Dennis wasn't going home empty handed.

His pal Collin Surbert agreed to help him build it at his Imperial Speed Equipment facility. "It's a 45-minute drive from my place. It became our Sunday ritual. I'd collect parts all week, drive out there on Sunday, and Collin's wife Elia would cook for us while we worked. I pictured exaggerated but balanced proportions. I always liked cartoonie styling and a tight fit, a car that hugs you while you drive it."

With those guidelines in mind, Dennis and Collin dragged the expired Touring inside and reanimated it. It was "modified" down to fighting weight and fitted with a 2x3-inch frame, kicked up 10 inches in front and 14 inches out back. The early Ford suicide front end employs right-hand-drive steering, "just for shits and giggles." A triangulated four-bar rear was added and it was engine time. Dennis' motto is, "If you want to go fast, build a flathead," but he couldn't stomach a bellybutton Ford. So a 1948 Caddy V-8 was set in front of the ubiquitous 1937 LaSalle trans and an 8¾-inch Mopar rear finished off the drivetrain. When Dennis and Collin couldn't source needed parts, they cast and machined them, in-house. The epitome of hardcore.

I caught up with the "Flat Cad Modified" just as Dennis was swapping his one-off tunnel ram tri-power intake for a blower, sitting on a custom cast manifold of his own design, with the old 3x2 setup now perched over the windmill. He was in the process of casting up the blower drive and tri-belt pulleys when we met. I was impressed, but not surprised. This is what usually happens when a long-suppressed desire finally sees the light of day. Everything gets lit up: the torch, the tires, and the driver's license points.

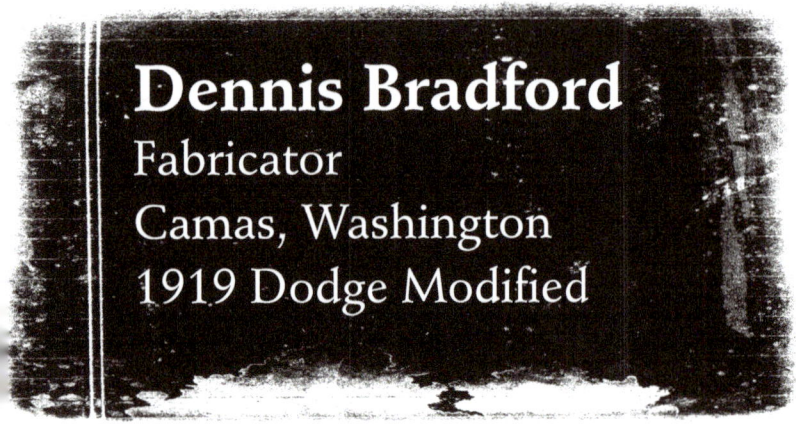

"I've learned so much since starting on this car. At least it's safe. I see kids building some really scary stuff out there! They should spend some time studying chassis design and learn to weld better."
(Photo Courtesy Collin Surbert)

Top: The focal point is the 1948 Caddy flathead mill. Hungry frogmouth scoops direct atmosphere into Stromberg 97s, through custom-cast tunnel ram, and into Caddy combustion chambers. Custom blower drive, manifold, and tri-power adapter were recently cast, so the Cad should be wheezed by the time you see this (note tri-belt blower drive crank pulley). Casting and machining was done at Collin Surbert's Imperial Speed Equipment. And that exhaust? This is where early flathead V-8 Ford racers stole the above-head exhaust idea. Cadillac was wise to head flow, but strangled it with restrictive manifolds. Dennis set the fumes free with home-built easy-exit tubes. A good ol' Cad/LaSalle transmission handles gear selection and an open-diff Mopar 8¾-inch rear uses 2.94:1 cogs to keep Dennis awake. "It makes so much torque! It blows off the tires in any gear." (Photo Courtesy Collin Surbert) *Bottom:* Garage-built 2x3-inch frame kicks up 10 inches in front and 14 inches in back. "Too much!" says Dennis. "It's hard to judge spring rates until the car's finished." That was an easy fix, though. A Model A front axle uses F-1 brakes, a buggy spring, and 1948 split 'bones to guide the hair blower through city traffic. Another transverse spring out back works with a home-built triangulated four-bar rig to handle Caddy torque. Right-hand-drive steering is a typical touch of Bradford whimsy, controlled by an F-1 box. Early Ford 15-inch truck wheels in front and late-model rears mount Hurst rubber all around. Dennis gives a sneak preview of blower presence here. It rides nice and goes straight and true. Until Dennis hammers it, then it's a curb kisser. (Photo Courtesy Collin Surbert)

CHAPTER 4: A NEW BREED OF EXTREME RODS   95

Dennis figures *two gauges are plenty.*
He can only read one at a time, *so why add the extra weight?*

Above: The remains of the 1919 Dodge Touring made excellent Modified fodder. The original lower-half windshield acts as wind fairing. The 1948 Cadillac radiator lost a few inches off the top tank to clear the Model A radiator shell. Swap meet headlights show the way. Everything from the doors back was hand crafted, including the oval fuel tank. A solo Model A taillight and license plate completes accessorization. Most people don't see past the engine anyway, deeming this nonessential info. Regarding Dennis' race number—the Dodge is neither half assed, nor half fast. (Photo Courtesy Collin Surbert) *Facing Page (top):* The little Dodge's stubby profile evokes bulldog stance and attitude. But Dennis insists, "It has 2 more inches of wheelbase than a Model A." Packaging and proportion is everything. Dennis was already having trouble seeing around the tri-power. Looking past the 4-71 huffer will be twice as challenging, twice as nerve wracking for passengers, and twice as much fun for Dennis' right foot. (Photo Courtesy Collin Surbert) *Facing Page (middle):* Dennis wanted a snug fit and he got it. Passengers are grateful for security provided by close quarters when Dennis rockets them through town in "the wrong side of the car." There's no steering wheel or brakes over there—a true test of faith. The upholstered seat helps (pucker up!). The steering wheel, a re-bent LaSalle shifter and stainless engine turned dash, built from an old refrigerator door provide welcome distractions. (Photo Courtesy Collin Surbert)

Dennis (below left) credits Collin (below right) with "taking me in the right direction," during the one-and-a-half-year build.

Dennis: "You s'pose Elia has dinner ready yet?"
Collin: "Yeah, probably."
Dennis: "Then this photo shoot is over. Let's eat!"
(Photo Courtesy Collin Surbert)

CHAPTER 4: A NEW BREED OF EXTREME RODS

Dylan Patterson
Musician
Minneapolis, Minnesota
1929 Ford Tudor

Looking every bit the part of an early Midwest B/Gas contender, Dylan's sedan was specifically influenced by local favorite Mike Strusinski's *Flathead's Revenge* D/Altered, campaigned by the Dualateers club since the late 1950s— "The toughest looking car I've seen." Despite the blown small-block Chevy with open headers and no radiator (it's actually hidden at the rear of the car), Dylan's version sees more street duty than strip action. "I haven't raced it on the strip, but around town, it sure goes!" It's no highway stranger either, accruing road rash en route to events near and far—a true real-world driver.

So how did this guy get from the grandstands to the driver's seat? "I learned the fabrication basics in high school and began building anything I could get my hands on." Dylan got his mitts on this A-bone via his pal Jeff "Titus" Bloedorn, who even threw in his own shop, to sweeten the deal. "He let me build it there in his garage and helped me make the transition from novice fabricator to hot rod builder." Two-and-a-half years later, the Tudor rolled out under the power of a single 4-barrel 283—"Simple and drivable." Dylan hit the road to the Hunnert Car Pileup ("About 450 miles") and the fun was on. At least until the return trip, when he lost a cylinder. "I had to constantly stop to clean the spark plug and refill the oil. About 3 gallons of oil and 11 hours later, we made it back alive."

The ensuing rebuild obviously incorporated a major upgrade in the intake department, with the addition of a GMC 6-71 huffer, topped with eight—count 'em, *eight*—Holley 94 carbs. What he lost in windshield visibility, he made up for in grins and period drag cred. You'd think this setup would drown the little mouse, but, "The induction system works pretty well on the street. I have plans for a different pulley set that will actually drive the blower to its potential. But it already scares me, as is!"

Dylan credits his hot rod mentors and peers with influencing the sedan's look and style. "I'm attracted to simplicity and honesty. I wanted to build a hot rod in its truest form, all motor and no frills." That's simple and honest enough for me.

"Don't get hung up in the terms and classifications of hot rodding. Just have fun and be true to yourself." (Photo Courtesy Scott Parkhurst)

Eight 94s should be enough to feed a 283, right? The air/fuel mix gets compressed by a GMC 6-71. The three-belt drive is a fun touch. Inside are forged pistons, but it's otherwise mostly stock, excepting the straight headers (musicians dig pipes). The wheezed mouse is backed by a trusty TH350 and 2.73:1-geared GM 10-bolt rear ("Great for highway speed adventures"). Considering the minimal weight of the Tudor body and spartan interior, this combo should pull hard enough to make Mike Strusinski nervous. (Photo Courtesy Scott Parkhurst)

Dylan runs the show from this distraction-free office (below), which he shares with the fuel tank. Strictly business in here. 'Flaked wheel and seats are blingy; otherwise, you get a shifter, pedals, and temperature gauge, the end. If noise, fumes, heat, and bone-jarring vibes aren't your idea of a luxury interior, you might want to toss this and select something from Oprah's Book Club. (Photos Courtesy Scott Parkhurst)

CHAPTER 4: A NEW BREED OF EXTREME RODS 99

Top: A tail shot reveals radiator cooling vents disguised as lightening holes and another glimpse of interior. Dylan flies his Lucky Bastards CC plaque proudly (plus it's bonus ballast). (Photo Courtesy Scott Parkhurst)

Middle: Traditional front suspension employs Ford gears from the 1940s. Dylan says a thorough rebuild of these components is next on his list ("Those Minnesota roads sure are hard on a hot rod!"). Gotta love the drag-only look of an empty radiator shell. Gold paint details the highlight features, while nailing the era. Dylan did his homework here. (Photo Courtesy Scott Parkhurst)

Bottom: An aggressive stance gives the sedan the appearance of launching off the line, even when posing for photos with its breath held (ignition off). A big chunk of the attitude developed when the body was chopped 6½ inches and channeled over the (modified) stock rails. The top is currently being redone by Dylan. I hope he leaves the drilled visor; it looks mean and let's face it, he can use the peep holes! (Photo Courtesy Scott Parkhurst)

Facing Page: Modern day hot rod hooligan Dylan Patterson spends his days thrashing, then panics to the nearest nightclub, where he wails until closing time with bleeding fingers. The American spirit is safe and sound, thank you. (Photo Courtesy Scott Parkhurst)

CHAPTER 4: A NEW BREED OF EXTREME RODS

Bob Johnson
Mechanic
Ramsey, Minnesota
1929 Ford Coupe

Bob and his brother Scott got so stoked upon seeing their first rat that they fried rubber all the way home to their pole barn shop and thrashed their cars together over the course of a brutal six-month Midwest winter. "The pole barn isn't insulated and we just had a small heater—it was F'n cold!" Tough sledding, indeed. If you've ever spun frozen wrenches with frozen fingers (and repeatedly bashed them into frozen steel) while lying on a frozen concrete floor after working all day, you know the passion of the Johnson brothers.

But the Johnsons persevered. Bob says, "It was a cold build, but we had a great time doing it!" While brother Scott put the screws to his mostly complete '31 coupe, manic mechanic Bob started with only a pair of rusty quarter panels. Bob's first order of business was sourcing the rest of the sheet metal (from buddies and swap meets) until he had enough tin to mock up something resembling a Model A. "It was nice, because the rust matched on all the panels!"

With the body on the floor, Bob set a dropped tube axle in front and an S-10 rear end in back and stood back to check proportions. Satisfied, he fired up his trusty welder and buzzed together a custom frame with jumbo kick-ups front and rear, providing the low center of gravity and squat stance required of a gow job intended to handle at speed and look good doing it. Besides the S-10 rear and tube front axle, another scoff at tradition is rack-and-pinion steering—rats run free of rules, using better parts to do so. The body was chopped and channeled over the frame to punch a smaller hole in the air and provide the classic hot rod presence of elbow-size side windows.

All points between A and B were connected and Bob's rattle-A was ready to rumble. When the spring thaw arrived, so did the Johnson Brothers, rolling their A-bones into town with the roar of new life and grins of satisfaction. Bob again: "I like it the way it is. I built it from pieces and not many guys can say that."

Today, Bob and Scott run their As all over creation, hitting "at least one car show a week." And since surviving six months in the deep freeze, they don't flinch at a little chill in the air, either: "Yeah, we drive 'em in the winter sometimes, too." Obviously, the heat of passion can warm even the most frigid bones. Even a frozen A-bone!

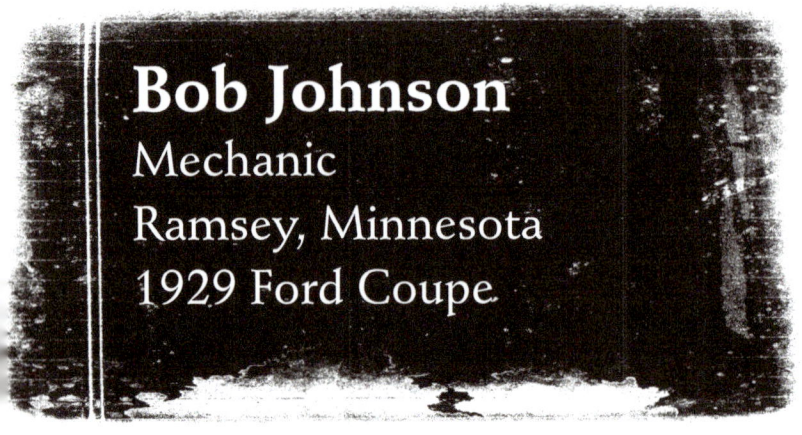

"If sparks don't fly, it's way too high! The coupe turns me on because it's low and fast!" (Photo Courtesy Scott Parkhurst)

Above: Bob's brother Scott bought a nearly complete coupe body from a guy raising money for a ring to go on his girlfriend's finger. Scott uses 200-inch Ford six-in-a-row go to make the show with Bob at Midwest hot spots. The Johnsonmobiles are near identical twins, with Scott opting for steelies and 1949 Dodge taillights. Both fly Frankensteiners colors. (Photo Courtesy Scott Parkhurst) *Below:* If the build story doesn't give you enough chills, the finished stance is sure cool enough to give you the shivers! A 5-inch chop and 3-inch channel over home-built frame, Z'd 3 inches in front and 14 inches in rear, results in athletic stance. Steroidal, even. The 3-inch dropped tube axle on a buggy spring uses 1953 Chevy brakes and 1935 Ford wire wheels on wide whites to scramble through traffic, while The 1937 Studebaker headlights lead the way. Rack-and-pinion steering (hidden under radiator) and S-10 rear end step away from tradition, into reality. It's definitely a driver and rarely gets any rest. (Photo Courtesy Scott Parkhurst)

Top: The 350/350 combo between the rails makes plenty of reliable power. A set of 3.54:1 gears in the Chevy 10-bolt rear ensure coupe is always in acceleration mode. Bob made his own headers and obviously has a gift for scoring swanky 1950s trim, like the 1952 Packard cowl scoop. (Photo Courtesy Scott Parkhurst) Bottom: Bob got pretty creative inside too, employing a 1959 Chevy gauge cluster as the focal point. A GM column, aftermarket wheel, and shifter are swap meet finds. Radio and pinstripes provide extra audio-visual stimulation, like Bob needs more of that! (Photo Courtesy Scott Parkhurst)

See-ya-later view shows off Rat-L-Trap's signature 1949 Chrysler taillights.

Ancient Dodge Power Wagon cowl lamp, converted to third brake light and ribbed S-10 Blazer top insert complete rear mods. This kind of image can stick with you like a tongue on a frozen header tube (or a hot one, for that matter). (Photo Courtesy Scott Parkhurst)

Craig Lankki
Tattoo Artist
Coon Rapids, Minnesota
1929 Ford Tudor

He walks the walk and lives the life. A hardcore biker and longtime tattoo artist, Craig Lankki's journey has been loud, fast, and colorful in all regards. But today, Craig owns Captive Elements Piercing and Tattoo in Blaine, Minnesota. For years, he commuted on a series of wild-ass choppers, but some workdays demand the stately presence of a black sedan. Businessmen do have to consider their images.

So when a friend found himself in the doghouse after purchasing an interesting project car, Craig stepped in. "His wife felt he had enough cars and there was still bare sheetrock in their house. I didn't care much for the way the car looked, but thought something could be done. I joined the Frankensteiners, hoping someone in the club would have the knowledge and ability to help me. They sure did!" By now, you've seen enough of the Frankensteiners' work in this book to know they have solid skills. Combine that with Craig's passion and keen eye, and what happened next shouldn't surprise you.

In one month of nights and weekends, the kooky Altered-style novelty car was transformed into a righteous badass that can intimidate its way into the best parking spot at the tattoo parlor. "I got help from most of the club, but it couldn't have been done as quickly without Frankensteiners Tim, Zach, and Bob. And Wayland, my brother-in-law from Alaska, also came and lent a hand." They started by rebuilding the custom frame, then transferred the early Ford suspension and GM drivetrain from the donor car. Before they could fit the new Tudor body onto the chassis, a decision had to be made. "I liked the big-block and 4-speed. I always figured if you're going to have a car like this, you need to stick to basics, so no automatic for me. Keeping the 4-speed meant I wouldn't be channeling it, but that's okay with me."

The finished product defines "rat" in the eyes of many—a bona fide rat motor, backed by a 4-speed and mid-range gearing in a scruffy A-bone, long the working man's body shell of choice. It goes like stink, scares dogs and children, pisses off the neighbors, and makes cops salivate. Has Craig Lannki created the ultimate rat?

"Rat rods are the basic form of hot rodding, built in garages by regular people on a small budget. They've been around all along, but not in the numbers they are now. Love 'em or hate 'em, but we aren't going away." (Photo Courtesy Scott Parkhurst)

Top Left: The "before" shot was taken the day of the teardown in Craig's shop. This early A four-door body, cut down to size and fitted with the big block/4-speed combo, must have been a kick on the street! Craig tossed everything but the drivetrain and suspension and started over. Homemade hairpins appear pretty dainty here, but Craig deemed them beefy enough to re-use. (Lettering on windshield reads, "For Sale $500,000 firm." Craig stole this thing!) (Photo Courtesy Craig Lankki) Top Right: Later that day, Craig and the Frankensteiners narrowed it down to the useable parts and knew what they had to work with. Not too shabby, really. And neither is the shop! (Photo Courtesy Craig Lankki) Bottom: Day two and things are already looking up. Better already! But we can picture it chopped, in flat black. (Photo Courtesy Craig Lankki)

Before anyone had time to catch their breath, the sedan was making the scene.

Zach Kurth's ride (left) illustrates more than one way to spell *"A Tudor."*

Lankki's sedan exudes muscularity from rear flank.

This is one street brawler you don't want to tangle with, unless you're willing to get tattooed!

Chris Darland
Filmmaker/Chassis Fabricator
Medford, Oregon
1932 Chevrolet Roadster

Have you seen the slapstick hot rod short features on DivebombersGarage.com? Fun stuff. They're made at Chris' Hot Rodz, a down-home rod and custom shop by day, beer-fueled film studio after hours. Chris is now finishing his first feature film, *American Thrill Ride*, a tongue-in-cheek street racer farce, but with much taller production aspirations than his previous work. "Work" is the active ingredient here: Chris sleepwalks out to the shop every morning, thrashes all day, then toils late into the night on the movie. The only way to survive such a regimen with wits intact is to blow off steam whenever possible. The one way Chris knows to do that is behind the wheel. But first, he needed a new wheel.

From childhood, Chris saw roadsters as the definitive hot rods. Possessing the definition of a non-roadster budget, he built a Hot Wheels version instead (painting it flat black with candy green flames). Inspired and open to fate, a pair of 1932 Chevy coupe quarter panels and a 1932 Chevy roadster cowl were soon gifted to him. Chris promptly found a couple of doors on a rusted-out stovebolt pickup, snuggled up to a tree. He shortened the doors 4 inches and had himself a roadster body.

The car took form between shop hours and film editing, over a one-year period. Chris made his own 2x3-inch frame and got a deal on a Speedway dropped axle kit and a pair of coil-overs for the back. A friend's reject 1970 Cutlass happened to be fitted with a 455-ci V-8/TH-375 transmission combo and Chris snatched 'em up. Next thing, Chris is blasting down the road in his very own roadster. "I remember every little detail of that first drive, but the main thing was, I couldn't stop smiling!"

The Bowtie Deuce has been mobile every day since. It's a road tripper and around-town zipper, racking up solid mileage without incident. Well, except for that freeway trip to Redding: "The left front blew at 70 mph. Shrapnel was coming at my face, but in the end, all that happened was we pulled over and got it fixed." The perfect metaphor for a guy who calmly gets to wherever he's headed, obstacles be damned. Thanks for the inspiration, Chris!

"'Rat rod is the public's new word for hot rod. They don't really know the difference, so they don't know how many people they offend with it. Heh, heh, heh..."

Top: Upon arrival at Chris' Hot Rodz, we found the topless tin lizard sunning itself in the gravel driveway, surrounded by intriguing future project material. *Bottom Left:* This shop is spitting distance from Chris'. There's quite a little metal crafting community thriving in the neighborhood. We saw everything from rats to restos and metal sculpture being built in a two-block area. *Bottom Right:* At Chris' shop, the roadster sticks its nose out into the sun to highlight the Speedway front suspension. Chris figures he saved money on fab time by buying this setup in kit form, including axles, spindles, brakes, spring and shackles, steering arm and hairpins. Model A radiator shell is just along for the ride, a hitchhiker, going nowhere fast. We razzed Chris about the blingy rolling stock. His reply, "These wheels were given to me. They came from a Chevelle with a Ford rear end, so they matched my bolt pattern needs." Got it. And they're decidedly Hot Wheelsy, too.

CHAPTER 4: A NEW BREED OF EXTREME RODS   111

Top: Leaning against the wall like a delinquent, the Bowtie roadster shows off its ex-coupe tail. A cast aluminum fuel filler, chrome decklid hinges, 1950 Pontiac taillights, upside-down 1924 Dodge windshield frame, mystery headlights, and genuine radiator shell join the polished American Torq Thrust Ds and Thrush side pipes to offset the Blitz Black and Kawasaki candy green. Good sense of balance, Chris. *Bottom Left:* As usual, Chris was in the right place at the right time and copped this 1970 Oldsmobile 455, when a buddy had to bail out of it. The original Q-Jet hides under the chrome air cleaner and the clear distributor cap is utterly hypnotic, especially at night. Chris whipped up the headers, but the Rocket is otherwise dead stock (as far as you know). Bonus: It came with a TH-375, GM's rare intermediate trans, classed between the TH350 and TH-400. Rocket Power torque twists an 8.8-inch Lincoln 2.45:1 rear end, mounted with Alston ladder bars and coil-over shocks. Fun glimpse of Chris' handywork on frame and chassis here, too. *Bottom Middle and Right:* Step-in interior says everything Chris wanted to convey with this build. For starters, the only gauge in the 1932 Chevy dash is the fuel level, "Because I built this car to escape life's problems. I don't need a bunch of gauges making me nervous." He made his own door panels from 'flaked vinyl and added the leopard skin inserts for grins ("The material was really cheap!"). A swap meet Sun tach, B&M Star shifter, and deep-dish wheel are merely driving tools. Truckstop covers for VW seats and pull handles on Dodge windshield frame join casual bodywork to enforce mission statement.

It didn't take long to get antsy for some road action. Chris filled the 13-gallon tank (19 mpg is claimed) and found several inviting long, straight stretches.

I love this neighborhood!

Collin Surbert
Construction Worker
Washougal, Washington
1936 Ford Three-Window Coupe

The Northwest embodies a distinctly mystical atmosphere. So you might expect Collin's coupe to bend around corners or astral-project down the street. It doesn't. It's more magical than that.

At age 12, Collin was building motorcycles, but got sidetracked by Mopar muscle cars. "I was heavy into the Mopars for years, then moved on to vintage-style hot rod projects. I built a few before the '36, but this one is my favorite. I wanted a '36 three-window for years, but they seemed unobtainable. Price usually had something to do with it." In 1999, Collin and wife Elia found a derelict 1936 body shell at a swap meet. "I didn't want to spend the money, but Elia talked me into it. I know, it's usually the other way around, but she knew it was a good deal and how much I wanted one." That was the first miracle.

Collin conjured up a custom tube frame, with air bags in mind. "I built the car so when it was completely lowered it'd be a half inch off the ground." His Pentastar influences revealed themselves via a 331-ci Hemi, fronting an A833 4-speed. A 4-inch dropped axle on un-split 'bones up front and triangulated torque arms with Panhard bar in back suspend the car. The body was channeled 5 inches over the rolling chassis and the top chopped 2½ inches. 1940 Ford truck fenders all around join a 1940 grille, dash, and steering wheel to make the coach-built statement. Collin waved his magic wrench over the car for only four months to produce miracle number two.

Collin wanted to introduce the coupe at the Viva Las Vegas show. The traditional last-minute thrash actually lasted for 48 hours. Collin notes, "Fortunately, I had a bunch of friends, willing to pitch in on the final bodywork. Two whole days of bustin' your butt on a friend's car is a lot to ask of someone! We tried to leave the Wednesday morning before the show, but left late Wednesday night. We headed down the highway to Vegas for our test drive. Elia and I sang the same songs over and over to keep ourselves awake. We drove straight through and got to Vegas at 5:00 am on Friday. We parked the car and fell onto the bed. We made it!" A miraculous trifecta, from Collin Surbert, the wizard of odds.

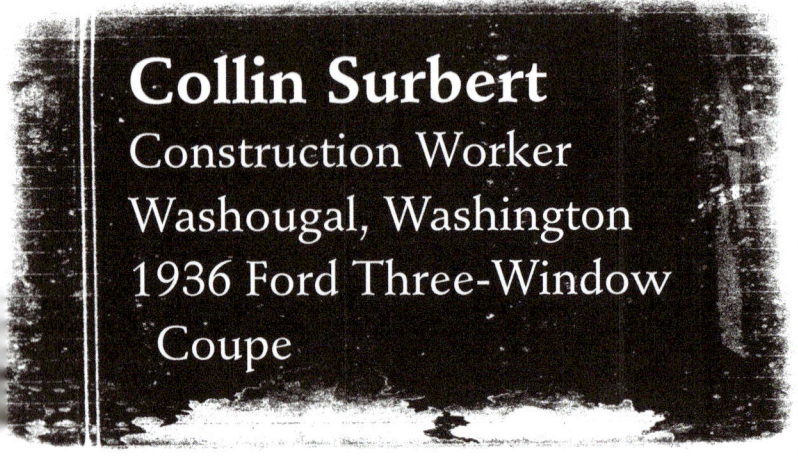

"My skills are self taught by observation, reading, and lots of good tips from people who know what they're doing." (Photos Courtesy Collin Surbert)

He exercised the bumper delete option and added de facto flame-thrower exhaust.

Top: The mobile Opium Den *plays the eyes, but is no hallucination. The deck lid really is welded shut, "For a smooth look." Collin crafted the fender skirts to resemble Lincoln flush-mounts. Check the fuel-fill door and license plate surround. Greek-style pinstripes by El Robbo and 1939 taillights are timeless over the DP90 paint. The coupe only appears to be melting into the asphalt and driving right through that wall. Typical hocus pocus from Collin's Imperial Speed Equipment shop. The coupe went from a rusted floorless shell to this, in four months. (Photo Courtesy Collin Surbert)* Bottom: *Snarky profile is result of mucho research and experience. Don't try this at home. At least not on anything as rare as a '36 three-window! Hard to believe these lines were produced with only a 2½-inch chop. More El Robbo teardrops draw attention to lowness, defining gravity of silhouette. Gentle curve along bottom edge lends air of motion, even when static. Collin says, "Hot rods aren't supposed to have hoods." But they can always use 1953 Olds Fiesta hubcaps. "I had to haul off a load of old refrigerator parts to get them for $10." They cover 15x5 1960 Ford pickup wheels. (Photo Courtesy Collin Surbert)*

Tailgaters beware
—Opium Den lights up regularly!

Left: C'mon in . . . 1940 steering wheels never go out of style, especially when accompanied by a 1940 dash! Collin pleads the Fifth, regarding furniture. "I have no idea what the seats came out of. I found them in a barn and they seem to work well." Fair enough. "My dad, Brian, fashioned the door panels from an old oriental rug," during the Great Viva Thrash of 2005. It figures this car would have a flying carpet. (Photo Courtesy Collin Surbert) *Right:* We love seeing customs with as much respect paid to the drivetrain as the exterior! The 1951 331-ci Chrysler Hemi is "basically stock" inside, but budget-correct external detailing adds so much to the coupe's overall presentation! The main event is the Edmunds intake, holding up the big Rochester 2-barrels. The function-equals-form cooling system drives the point home to a tweaked Tru-Cool aluminum sprint car radiator. Knowing there's an A833 4-speed behind all of this just lends even more street cred to the '36. Jeff Wolf's cowl striping frames Hemi surprise appropriately. (Photo Courtesy Collin Surbert)

(Photo Courtesy Elia Surbert)

Aile, Collin, and Elia Surbert with the family car. Elia sums it up, "I had to talk him into buying that body. He walked away from it several times and ran back again and again to evaluate it. It was a pile of junk, but the perfect candidate for what he wanted to do. He built it in four months and it's solid. He always says anything he builds will be safe and he'd be comfy putting me behind the wheel. I guess he really does love me." These shots will go right under Dad's and Grandpa's rides in the photo album. (Photos Courtesy Elia Surbert)

Patricio Germano
Computer Repair
Buenos Aires and San Andres, Argentina
1951 Ford Four-door Sedan

I don't even recall being in Buenos Aires, but I'm told I enjoyed myself. I apparently met Patricio Germano there. Upon returning home, I found some unexplainable items in my luggage, including blurry photos of elderly *cacharros* (American cars), patched together with spit and prayers, seemingly making their way through traffic to the graveyard. No wonder I made note of Patricio's story.

Facts to verify: Patricio works like a dog at a large computer retailer. His daily driver is a '68 Falcon (looks like an American '63). He slaps a mean standup bass in two bands (Hillbilly Rocket and Radio Texas). He and fiancée Analia share an apartment (I somehow owe them money for unspecified damages).

According to my notes, when Patricio heard of a shoebox Ford for sale within his price range, he and Analia hotfooted it over there. "Analia and I go to see the car in a 'not nice' town about 50 kilometers from my home, in my good old Falcon. It was night, on the outskirts of town. We saw it standing by an old barn, surrounded by several cars that were cut in half and parts everywhere. When we saw it, we fell in love." This was a running, driving car (complete, except for one radio knob) for $1,500 (U.S.). What's not to love? The shoebox was driven directly to San Remo Kustoms and Service, Uncle Daniel Ferrazin's repair and restoration shop. It's a very busy place, but Uncle Daniel hangs out the *"Perdon, Somos Cerrados"* sign ("Sorry, We're Closed") on Saturdays. That's because Saturday is a school day, with Professor Ferrazin conducting private fabrication classes for his star student, Patricio Germano.

The Saturday sessions produced dramatic results. The top was chopped; a two-door conversion performed; new floors, rockers, and multiple patch panels were fabbed and installed; along with rebuilds of the suspension and drivetrain. All of this, in one year of Saturdays. Patricio is a quick study, but is learning that fast isn't always best. "My uncle likes to do things the hard way. It's a lot of work, but what the hell? I'm saving a car from sure death and I'm making the coolest shoebox in Argentina!" And his graduation present, upon completing Uncle Daniel's Basic Training regimen? Well, there's the relationship with his uncle, who has offered Patricio a job at San Remo Kustoms and Service. And, oh yeah, a badass custom shoebox for his commute! The ultimate win/win/win!

"A group of young people and I are starting the fire of the custom culture movement (in Argentina). And yes, we do have modern tools, but we like to do it the old way." (Photo Courtesy Japo Santos)

Top Left: When I first asked Patricio for pictures of his car, this is what he sent. The artwork is by his girlfriend, Analia. Maybe my Spanish needs more work. (Photo Courtesy Patricio Germano) *Top Right* Patricio's classic "before" shot gives impression of cherry-pie granny-goer. Not even! Evil lurked just below the surface. A mechanical exorcism was necessary on each of thousands of rusted fasteners and panels. At least swearing sounds cooler in Spanish. (Photo Courtesy Patricio Germano) *Middle Left:* Curbside parking at San Remo Kustoms and Service. The shoebox was constantly pushed outside for updated perspective on flow and balance. Getting some fresh air to the brain doesn't hurt, either. (Photo Courtesy Analia Fretes)

Above and Right: The original 239-ci flathead V-8 came ready to rumble, just pour the gas and strike the spark. The standard (non-overdrive) 3-speed and rear end will stay for now. The flathead sounds angry and who could blame it? Can you imagine the life this thing has lived? It should get some expert nurturing now. Meanwhile, the body is taking shape in the background. (Photos Courtesy Patricio Germano)

CHAPTER 4: A NEW BREED OF EXTREME RODS 119

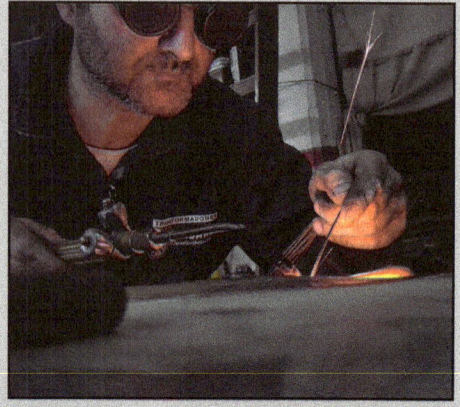

Top Left: It only looks like a medieval bondage device. This contraption is actually Uncle Daniel's clever way of checking measurements as work progresses, ensuring tight specs, side-to-side. It works great, too, pulling Patricio's sled back into shape after a car wreck and untold hours under the torch. (Photo Courtesy Analia Fretes) *Top and Middle Right:* Uncle Daniel's gas flame announces, "Class is in session!" Patricio grinds the day away, along with 50-plus-years worth of rust. (Photos Courtesy Analia Fretes) *Bottom Left and Right:* After hours, Patricio goes ballistic onstage (here with Mack Stevens at the San Pedro Music Festival), then winds down at neighborhood café with Analia. (Photos Courtesy Patricio Germano)

Top: Patricio was hot for air bags and a four-link rear. This took some doing, as shipping costs were even more inflated than the parts themselves. He did what he had to do and the shoebox was finally flattened. (Photo Courtesy Japo Santos) Bottom: The most recent update shot from Patricio. Rolled rear pan came out nice. "My short-term plans include rounded hood, door and trunk corners, bucket seats, nosed and decked with frenched headlights, lake-style pipes, a 1949 dash, and a DeSoto grille." You know he'll have fun getting there, but meanwhile, this doesn't suck too bad! (Photo Courtesy Japo Santos)

Chris Clark
Hot Rod Shop Office Manager
Portland, Oregon
1961 Morris Minor

Infamous Japanese character actor Godzilla raised hell on the streets of Tokyo, fathered a son, and disappeared—an all too common story these days. But reports of a similar creature rampaging through the Pacific Northwest spurred us to dispatch reporter Pompadour Polanski to Portland, Oregon. Pomp, what's the situation there?

"Scotty, I'm standing at this southeast Portland intersection, where minutes ago, witnesses reported a 'dark blur' moving at incredible velocity down this street—to my left here (Zoom in on the tire tracks, Larry)—leaving behind a 'foul scorched odor' and a trail of smoke (How's my hair look?). These are characteristics of Son of Godzilla, long believed by locals to be living underground in the shadows of the city. Portland police are investigating an eastside apartment the creature may have shared with iconic Northwest personality Sasquatch, but have released no details at this hour. Scotty?"

Thank you, Pompadour Polanski, in Portland, Oregon. Coming up on Newswatch Six: Are poodles using gamma rays to organize a takeover of your car club? Stay tuned . . .

I tracked down Chris Clark, owner of the Son of Godzilla Morris, in Portland. It's regularly mistaken for a small monster (thus the name), a VW Beetle, and a rat rod. Chris shrugs it all off with a chuckle, letting people think what they will.

The idea here is simply a fun street car and Lil 'Zilla delivers, wholesale. The power-to-weight ratio is beyond nuts, with a 550-plus-hp small-block Chevy V-8 pulling the 2,100-pound package around. The build budget was also lightweight, with $20 per week stretched over a 26-year span, so far. At that rate, it won't be "nice" anytime soon, but Chris is okay with that. After all, he's a family guy, with wife Sia and daughter Celina claiming first dibs on the paycheck.

Meanwhile, Chris torments the streets and sneaks off to the strip when possible. The Morris drives to the track, runs low 10s, and drives back home, with a "way wrong" torque converter. A recent swap to an appropriate converter should mean solid 9s by the time you read this. A ring-and-pinion swap was the only change required to run 140 mph at Bonneville, at half throttle ("Anything more and it spun"). Lil 'Zilla is a multi-purpose monster.

Just like its cranky father, Son of Godzilla was born to terrorize the populace and does it well. Chris says he's only along for the ride. At least that's what he tells cops and reporters.

"I admit to liking some cars that some people may deem a rat rod. But usually, those cars are teetering pretty close to the traditional hot rod overlap. The Morris is neither. It's just a street/strip car to me."

Chris uses the car as a pack mule, running errands and hitting all the hot spots while he's at it. Yeah, it's low—1½ inches at the bottom of the front fenders, which Chris de-crumples every few weeks. No air bags here; this is permanent ride height. Even with baffles in the collectors, it's still loud(!); broadcasting camshaft overlap near and far. The headlight covers (actually aluminum tractor shift lever covers) are Bonneville leftovers. Chris says, "Driving it on the street is actually a pain. Everybody wants to talk and I'm not very sociable to strangers."

Local residents alerted authorities to our noisy photo shoot, where a lengthy stand-off ensued, but I waited them out. Whew! The Morris is roughly 7/8 of a VW Beetle in size: small enough to be easily hidden, if necessary.

There's plenty of time to ponder your run at Bonneville, while waiting for the course to clear. Chris agrees, "Each time I sat at that starting line, I thought to myself, 'Clark, what the hell are you doing?!' But when I got the wave to go, it didn't matter." The 86-inch wheelbase wasn't a problem, as much as the wide rear tires. With 2.73:1 gears, it went 140, but pinballed so bad, Chris couldn't get past half throttle. "Salt Fever is real! The 140 pass had me tucking vinyl, but wanting more. By far, the most hair-raising ride was at Bonneville."

Left: The four-bolt 400 block (.030 inch over) uses a de-stroked Eagle forged crank, and H-beam rods to make 377 inches with 10.5:1 Keith Black forged slugs. A custom Isky solid flat-tappet cam works with custom Smith Brothers pushrods and Comp roller rockers. Home-ported Dart Pro 1 heads receive A/F cocktail from a hogged-out Edelbrock Street Tunnel Ram supporting two Holley 650 double pumpers, dug out of mud after a drag boat crash. Headers are homemade: 1⅛-inch primaries dump into 3½-inch collectors (with baffles for street use). Fun details like homemade fuel block (mounted with 1932 Ford steering wheel spokes), homemade linkage, and drilled manifold support are typical 'Zilla details. New (for 2011) 5800 stall TCI 8-inch converter spins in home-built Powerglide (with trans brake), herding horses to 8¾ Mopar rear loaded with 3.91:1 gears on a Strange spool and Dutchman axles. The 1965 T-Bird radiator tries to cool it. *Middle:* Chris' command center is furnished in aluminum from a trailer house that washed downstream in a flood (I told you this was a budget build). The Hurst shifter and MSD ignition are the only store-bought items, everything else is homemade or swap meat (steering wheel, Stewart Warner gauges, and seats). Dash hinges down for distributor access and hey, it even has cup holders. (Crucial for summer cruising in tin interior!) A teensy gas pedal is hidden beside Opel steering column. *Right:* Typical interior decorating for Chris—shifter handle is swap meet starter handle (used on blown fuelers), cut down and drilled for shifter. I imagine the late Jim Davis would be okay with this.

Lil 'Zilla has tortured tracks around the country. It's playing at Champion Raceway in Medford, Oregon, in these shots of a 10.36 run. On running the quarter, Chris says, "Everything seems to go away. Amazing how nothing else matters. The stands disappear and all I see is my lane." The launch can get rowdy, then 'Zilla hunkers down and goes straight as a string. Really.

En route to an undisclosed location for some testing. Yeah, the scoop is distracting. Chris is used to it now, but confesses, "The first time I drove it, that engine in the windshield was huge!"

Sergey Sadovnik
Bus Mechanic
Odessa, Ukraine
1967 Likhachev ZIL-157

Sergey does his spark throwing and rubber burning in chilly Ukraine and is having an absolute blast, thank you very much. Apparently, this is how far away from American culture you have to go to escape the bastardization of rodding. We give lip service to old-time hot rod ideals in the States, but Sergey is living those values in real time. Yeah, he uses Auto Cad computer programs to solve design and engineering riddles, and a good ol' MIG welder to stick things together. But as for raw materials, Sergey worked with what was available. In this case, that's Soviet-era military truck parts. "The ZIL-157 cabin and grille were purchased from a friend. She lay long in his garden. Motor and gearbox were purchased from the big garage for buses where I work. Director of the bus park is also named Sergei (and is my friend). He acted as godfather of my project. He does passionate restoration of Soviet military equipment. Therefore, we have a lot of these parts. If not for him and his hobby, *Iron Head* could not be born." As per hot rod tradition, he modified what he had and made about everything else from scratch. He did all this in a dank tin building on the edge of town, with the icy Black Sea lapping at the shop door all winter (which uses up most of the calendar).

"Project *Iron Head*" is the tag for Sergey's marching deuce-and-a-half, and I find it fitting. You don't pull off this kind of accomplishment without a tenacious belief in your passion. Check out Sergey's photos, read the captions, sit back, close your eyes, and imagine yourself in his place.

Then ask yourself, would it be worth it to you?

"In my project, I proceed from the principles which were used by the first builders of hot rod—use the available technology and materials. I really like what I do and I do not want to stop. In my head, [I have] a lot of projects." (Photo Courtesy Irina Pichugin)

"After *Iron Head* is tested on the road, I intend to **disassemble the machine** and remove all **flaws**.

There will be **plenty of work.**"

Artist's rendering of a stock ZIL. (Photo Courtesy Sergey Sadovnik)

These are the first photos of the finished product (save for interior), fresh from the shop. The cab and grille are 1967 ZIL—2½-ton Soviet multi-purpose vehicles, favored by the Red Army up to 1979. Sergey understates, "I use a heavily modified cab of this truck. Now is a period of pure art and intuition." He cut it into 12 pieces and reassembled with reckless abandon—chopped 6 inches, narrowed 13 inches, sectioned 8 inches, and sliced 4 inches off the bottom. It's channeled about 5 inches over the frame rails. Cab height was reduced from 60 inches to 42 inches. The bed was fabbed from scratch. Sergey mocked it up for our photos, then tore it back down. (Photos Courtesy Irina Pichugin)

The 260-ci V-8 originally powered a GAZ-66 Soviet military 4x4 COE, built by the Gorky Automobile plant from 1962 to 1995. Original output was 135 hp, and Sergey's isn't new anymore. It's assisted by a GAZ-66 4-speed manual trans, featuring synchro third and fourth gears. Motor mounts testify to Sergey's fun level on this build. (Photo Courtesy Irina Pichugin)

CHAPTER 4: A NEW BREED OF EXTREME RODS

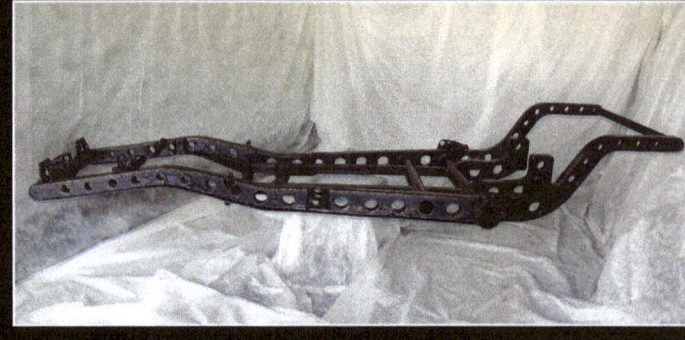

"The frame, springs, lever shocks, seats, exhaust, steering system, and rear axle I took out the off-road vehicle GAZ-69." This model ceased production in 1972. Sergey kicked the rails up in a graceful radius, Swiss cheesed and sleeved them, built the I-beam front axle from steel sheet, and employed GAZ parts where he could. Sergey fabbed a stout triangulated two-bar to locate rear end ("A handy layout, and compact") and beefy four-bars up front. All crossmembers and bracketry were home-built, of course. The craftsmanship is first-rate. The weird black chassis paint was a botched rubberization attempt. "The result is a failed experiment. I will sand and repaint the frame." (Photos Courtesy Irina Pichugin)

Iron Head *guards the shop while on standby for the next test drive. Regarding the hot rod scene in eastern Europe, Sergey says, "Only I do it here. Unfortunately, in Ukraine and Russia, nobody likes problems. There are projects easier (than mine), but I love what I do." (Photo Courtesy Irina Pichugin)*

Although fiercely independent, Sergey (right) expresses gratitude for help and encouragement from pal Sergei Golodny (left). (Photo Courtesy Irina Pichugin)

Sergey and daughter Anistasia roll Iron Head *back into the shop after a day's thrash. (Photo Courtesy Irina Pichugin)*

"Tomorrow we install the interior."

Chapter 5
SHOCK VALUE WITH A GRIN
—OH YEAH?!

Randy Ellis' 1945 Willys CJ-2a Jeep.
(Photo Courtesy Christian Hazel)

GET A LOAD OF THIS

H
ot rodders turned the one-upmanship game into an Olympic event from day one. That's just human nature, I suppose.

In Ratville, it culminates in how low you can go; too many carbs is a good start; does this exhaust make my ass look fat; envelope shredding proportions; Buck Rogers parts sourcing; obscure engine contest winners; and graphics banned by the DMV. In most rodding niches, less is more. But once a rat infestation hits town, too much is never enough. The objective is to shake the troops from complacency, lest history repeat itself. And the rats are right on target.

The innocence of the original anything-for-a-laugh manifesto is breached occasionally by misguided interlopers who are promptly dismissed for missing the point. Don't take yourself or your car too seriously. This is a party, not a competition. No wagering, please. There are plenty of other automotive pursuits where keeping score and obeying rulebooks are respected. This ain't one of them.

Okay, so competitiveness is human nature. And hey, rats are people too, you know. If you can make your buddy blow beer through his nose upon spotting your new alternator bracket, or make your girlfriend pee herself when you debut that hidden nitrous system, congrats on being goal oriented.

Are these guys serious about this stuff? Well, ask a silly question and this is what you get . . .

Brent Holloway's '31 Ford sedan.
(Photo Courtesy Brent Holloway)

Robert Killian
Retired Mechanic
Canton, Georgia
1928 Ford Tudor

Rats have infested dragstrips since the first hot dog stand opened, but few have presented a display of shock and awe to equal Robert Killian's gonzo Model A. Soft spoken and unassuming, Robert is actually one of a severely deranged few who hang it all out on the 1,320-foot stage, where the clocks aren't impressed with imagery and attitude. Driving this heap to and from the track just makes the cheese at the finish line all the sweeter. Yep, the head and taillights aren't just there for extra ballast, this is a good-old-fashioned street/strip beater. (Robert clarifies, "We probably won't drive it more than 50 miles, each way.")

That's one goal anyway, the other being 6-second/200-mph timeslips. Robert wants to score both goals in a genuine, steel-bodied A-bone, with no blower, injectors, or nitro. He's getting there with gasoline and carburetors in an 83-year-old car.

Of course, those carbs are Pro/Stock-influenced split Dominators, riding around on an 820-ci Jon Kaase–built Ford Hemi, fronting a Pro/Mod-style Powerglide transmission in a chrome-moly South East Hot Rods (SEHR) SFI 25.2-spec double-rail chassis. Robert really wants that cheese!

Initial testing at nearby Paradise Drag Strip produced strong and straight launches and some typical teething issues. Builder/crew chief Steve Tucker reports, "It did track nice and straight, which was a concern on my end." Robert's take was the deciding factor, "It felt every bit as good as my old Pro/Stock car!" So two weeks later, the show went to NHRA's Hot Rod Reunion at Bowling Green, Kentucky, where "Uncle Jed" stepped up to 8.08 seconds at 177 mph on a rain-weeping track. Not a bad start.

True, this isn't Robert's first gow job. He started wrenching at a Ford dealership while still in high school. That experience led to Killian Motorsports, where "Ford factory guys would come around" sniffing for hot tips. A long string of fast Fords evolved into four years of IHRA mountain motor Pro/Stock racing. The connection with legendary Ford engine guru Jon Kaase came with the territory.

The sedan was screwed together at Steve Tucker's South East Hot Rods in Ballground, Georgia, "which is a little 30- by 40-foot-square shop out behind his house in the hills," confides Killian. Steve (a retired firefighter) does it just as much for love, as money. Probably more for the love.

By the time you read this, Killian's jalopy will likely be the most rapid rodent on planet Earth. The hook is that it's operated by the two most laid-back, southern gentlemen I've ever met. How can that be?

The locals call it "Mountain Magic."

"Everybody wants to put a car in a category. I say, 'To each his own.' This is a rolling heap. It just rolls really fast!" (Photo Courtesy Jason Cole)

Body is cherry, other than the chop and rear wheelwell clearancing.

Top Left: The patina is honest. It should make a statement pulling into the burger joints like thousands of Model As before it. This one might stick in the memory banks a little longer than most though. (Photo Courtesy Robert Killian) Top Right: At the track, railbirds will be yacking up the Model A body, but here in Ratville, the engine is the jaw dropper. In the early days of IHRA mountain motor Pro/Stock, Jon Kaase discovered Ford big-blocks accepted more bore and stroke than anything else, so that's what he built. Today, that knowledge manifests itself in this 820-ci chunk of Dart CNC'd billet aluminum, wearing Kaase hemispherical heads. SEHR stainless step headers (2 to 2¼ to to 2½ inches) use Burns mufflers. It's backed by an ATI Powerglide and 8-inch 4500 stall converter, spinning a Mark Williams carbon fiber driveshaft in a Pro/Mod-style housing. Nothing is left to chance at this level (1,930 hp, according to Kaase's dyno). Moroso four-stage dry sump system pumps lifeblood. Reciprocating assembly, head, and valvetrain specs are "top secret." (Photo Courtesy Steve Tucker) Bottom: What's it take to launch an A-bone like a rocket, then bring it back to earth like a magnet? Steve Tucker's moly double-rail chassis carries an SFI 25.2 certification sticker, same as a Pro/Modified. This is probably the first I-beam front-axle car the chassis cert guy ever affixed such a tag to. That axle is a Super Bell aluminum model, sporting Pete & Jakes alloy shocks, Mark Williams carbon fiber brakes, and Mickey Thompson rubber on Billet Specialties 15x4 wheels. At the opposite end of the 130-inch wheelbase, Mark Williams supplied the 9½-inch rear end, employing 40-spline gun-drilled axles, spun by 3.90:1 gears on a spool. More carbon fiber brakes and a pair of Stroud chutes ensure Robert's trips all have happy endings. M/T 33x10.5Wx16 slicks on 16x16 Billet Specialties hoops supply enough grip to make denture wearers jealous. Weight is 2,805 pounds, with driver—2,635, without. Robert demonstrates at Bowling Green in this photo. (Photo Courtesy Jason Roberson)

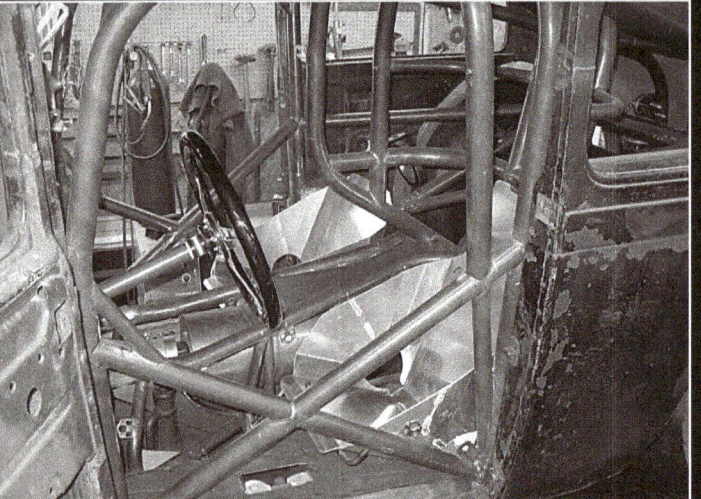 

Left: Hidden within SEHR jungle gym rollcage are Hurst Quarter Stick shifter, Autometer gauges, a steering wheel, driver, harness, some switches, and not much else. Note Pro/Mod-style driveshaft housing. SEHR did all the tinwork in here, as well as the 10-gallon fuel cell, wings, wheelie bars, "and about a thousand other things." (Photo Courtesy Steve Tucker) *Right:* Keeping good company in the pits at the Hot Rod Reunion in Bowling Green, Kentucky, where Uncle Jed entered A/Gas. Besides nostalgia drags, Robert will also run Top Sportsman. He describes T/S as "kind of a fast bracket class," with dial-ins from 6.30s to 7.20s, roughly. Chances are, this will be the only entry driven into the pits when the gates open in the morning. (Photo Courtesy Jason Roberson)

The sedan was named for Jed Clampett. The "Mountain Magic" moniker refers to Kaase and Killian's racing backgrounds and is also a nod to local geography. The "Speed Shop" was an afterthought to shame poseurs using fake shop names on the doors of their street cars. Robert has some cool street cars himself (including another A sedan) and sees no need to present them as something they're not. (Photo Courtesy Jason Roberson)

Brent Holloway
Electrical Contractor
Golden, Colorado
1931 Ford Sedan

For those demanding a definition of rat rods, here ya go—the prototypical rat. The Holloway Model A is your textbook example, with all the boxes checked off—thrashed together with traditional elements and whatever else was handy, and assembled with a bold whimsy. Driven hard and put up wet, then cast aside to make way for fresh meat. Repeatedly.

The sedan was originally built by Brent Holloway in 2007. This freeform example of vermin expressionism was quickly sold to finance the next project and forgotten. Since then, it's had more names on the title than I could track. Each new caretaker put his own personal stamp on the sedan, enjoyed it for a while, and moved on. I caught up with it briefly, and then it was gone again.

In 2008, it found its way to Jamie Lane and Kelli Smotherman's Franklin, Tennessee, garage, where it was re-wired after catching fire on the initial test drive, fitted with custom headers that eventually puked the baffles out (never to be replaced), received twin fuel tanks made from fire extinguishers, had the front suspension and cooling system rebuilt, was driven at every opportunity, was photographed by Richard Fleener, and finally sold to Indy Racing League hotshoe, Paul Tracy.

Tracy had been battling his way through the 2009 IRL season—intense and stressful. He longed for a getaway car to relax with on his rare free days, but had no time to build one. So when he caught wind of the Holloway lab rat, he was on it. After a snappy remodel at Performance Motorsports in Las Vegas, the steam valve was opened wide. Alas, reality even caught up with speedy Paul Tracy. Mike Fisk, from Performance Motorsports told me, "Paul loved it and loved driving it, but he didn't have the time to drive it anymore. He gave it up for the new owner to put his touches on it and have fun with it." And the cycle continues. It's still out there somewhere, living underground.

Best viewed through eyes with a respect for creative freedom and a cold, hard, focus on reality, rats are tin gypsies and just as sexy. In fact, you can even liken rats to porn queens—some of them prefer to be considered "actresses," but those few who proudly proclaim to be "porn stars" are typically more fun to watch. Likewise, the Holloway A wags its tail proudly, celebrating all that is liberating about rat culture. For all that it was, what it is, and what it isn't yet, I proclaim the Holloway A to be King Rat! Of this collection, anyway.

"I just thought, 'What can I do to make something cool?' My buddy Cadillac Bob built one kinda like this and I said, 'I'm gonna do one, smaller and cooler.'" (Photo Courtesy Richard Fleener)

Top Left and Right: Exclusive build shots from Brent's personal collection reveal birthplace of Holloway A (Holloway Hot Rods) and birthing methods employed by Brent. "The body was sectioned 10 inches, channeled 4 inches, and chopped 8 inches. All the bodywork was brazed with oxy/acetylene." Brent built a 2x4-inch frame, added 1960 Ford front axle on split 1940 'bones and a 12-bolt rear, all on air bags. Coddington 20- and 22-inch Spider wheels rolled it. Holloway decided to run the billet dubs, "to stir up some shit among the haters." It worked! The nose was made from 1949 International hood on 1937 Ford grille. "And north Denver fence pickets were used for the roof." (Photos Courtesy Brent Holloway) Middle Left and Right, and Bottom: Jamie Land says, "I'm 6 feet, 3 inches, so it wasn't very comfortable for me. But it was still a blast to drive! Well, until you parked it, then the crowd wouldn't let you get away." Today, Jamie and Kelli roll in a '59 Chevy Biscayne. "It's a lot more comfortable." Jamie replaced Brent's single 1960 Buick "afterburner" taillight with these Caddy jobs and added louvered panel to dispel radiator BTUs. (Photos Courtesy Richard Fleener)

Graphic evidence of just how **shrunken** the sedan really is.

Parked alongside photographer Richard Fleener's '59 El Camino, which has been lowered itself. Imagine flying down the freeway, looking up to see yourself reflected in tractor-trailer hubcaps. (Photos Courtesy Richard Fleener)

Since waving goodbye to the Holloway car, Jamie and partner Kelli have built a couple more Model A sedans, so they're still in the game. (Photo Courtesy Richard Fleener)

Top Left and Middle: The Paul Tracy makeover took place at Performance Motorsports in Las Vegas. The 5-speed made way for an automatic, the dubs were swapped for vintage styled ET-IIIs and the tired 307 was traded for a 350 with an Edelbrock tunnel ram and a pair of Holleys. Randy Cothran at PM alludes, "It wasn't set up quite right when it came here." (Photos Courtesy Richard Fleener) *Top Right:* Brass upholstery makes a dramatic statement to onlookers and passengers alike. Jamie says, "The engine heat comes at you from the front and the fans blow the radiator heat at you from behind. It'll about burn you outa there." We're guessing that's an understatement. But it didn't stop Jamie and Kelli from driving it to Nashville and Murfreesboro. Although Jamie concedes, "We went up Franklin Road and stayed off the freeway." A rocker arm welded to rebar makes a unique shifter for the T-5. (Photo Courtesy Richard Fleener) *Bottom Left and Right:* Brent stays too busy to miss the sedan. His fleet of 40-plus cars sees to that. On the Model A, "I feel honored that an Indy Car driver wanted something I built. My thoughts on the improvements? If they make it more drivable, like the automatic trans that Paul put in, fine. I don't like the Caddy taillights the Tennessee guy put in. Maybe it'll be discovered in a barn in 50 years? Meanwhile, I plan to build more cars." Thanks, Brent. (Photos Courtesy Brent Holloway)

Randy Ellis
Chassis Fabricator
Phoenix, Arizona
1945 Willys CJ-2A Jeep

Phoenix houses more than a million citizens, outnumbered three-to-one by sagacious Gila monsters, tequila-guzzling rattlesnakes, and blues-crooning coyotes sporting neckerchiefs (well, if you eat enough peyote buttons, anyway). So it just figures that this is Randy's idea of an appropriate around-town driver. Maybe he just wanted to blend in?

The first impression of the Jeep prompts the same question from everyone: Who is this guy and where is he coming from? Tell 'em, Randy: "I started tearing things up at a real young age, so I also learned how to fix them. My dad got me started with paint and body and taught me to do a complete frame-up restoration on my first car, a '69 RS Camaro. I was 12, and I still have the car. I was on my fourth 4x4 by the time I graduated high school. I started doing some extreme four wheeling, really pushing equipment and increasing what was needed to stay on top. I ended up running a fab shop for eight years before starting my own in 2000. I love building suspensions and chassis, from rock crawlers to desert race trucks, monster trucks to drag cars."

He built the Jeep during a rare lull in the action at Randy Ellis Design, where they crank out custom-fabbed 4x4 trucks and accessories. The shop would be somewhat quiet for five weeks (after hours, anyway) and that's exactly how long it took Randy to perform his unique brand of telekinesis on the Jeep, from start to finish. "Building race cars over the past years has taught me not to waste time. There was a show in Las Vegas and the Jeep had to be done in time to drive it there. I finished the car with the last stencil still wet and drove it to Vegas in time to register!"

I'm not surprised that a guy like Randy had an old Jeep laying beside the shop, or even that he could build it so fast, but nobody was ready for what rolled out five weeks later. Randy was just chasing a vision. "I thought how odd and cool it would be to see what *should* be 2 feet off the ground—chopped and dropped, with a custom chassis to support it all." A visionary desert rat (or Clairvoyant Sonoran Rodentia).

"I'd built a few hot rods over the years and thought the rat rod deal was pretty cool. My Jeep used to be a rock crawler. I'm just an off-road guy that wanted a rat rod."

(Photo Courtesy Vic Macias)

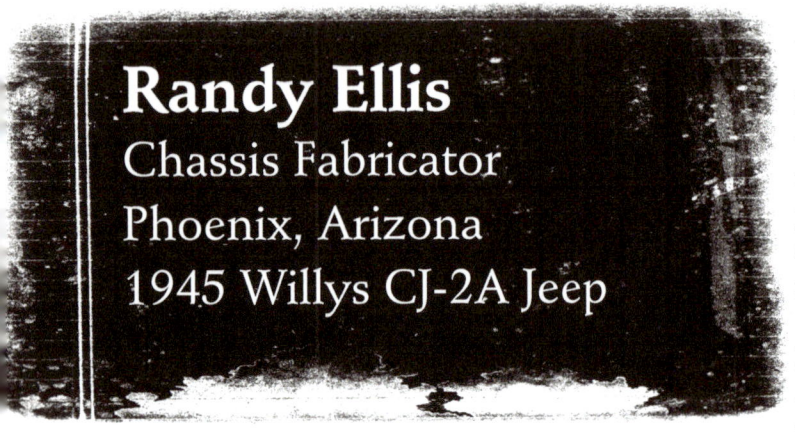

Top: I've witnessed the unexplainable in the desert, but this just seems right—a boy and his toy, stirring up their own private dust devil. Breathtaking, when observed in their natural habitat. Actually, this was meant to be a posed shot, but a scorpion crawled up Randy's throttle leg. (Photo Courtesy Christian Hazel) *Bottom:* Randy's 2x3-inch frame holds up a Randy Ellis Design I-beam axle on cantilevered air bags and an R.E.D. four-bar. A '77 Chevy 1/2-ton truck donated many parts, including spindles, hubs, rotors, and calipers. Psychedelic drag link emanates from custom steering box by Benchworks, employing GM, Ford, and Mopar components. A 12-bolt rear on more of Randy's trick cantilevered bag mounts is located with another R.E.D. four-bar system. KYB front shocks and Rancho rears help make emergency landings survivable. Best part is that it all works perfectly together—the old '45 is king of any hill it aspires to fly off. (Photo Courtesy Christian Hazel)

Top Left: One-off beadlock-style wheel by R.E.D. matches air cleaner lid and glovebox door. Bestop seats, hand-grenade knob on custom shifter, and Stewart Warner gauges are about all the news in here. (Photos Courtesy Randy Ellis Design) *Top Middle:* The donor truck's drivetrain pulls the flyweight Jeep like a locomotive (heavy on the loco!). After a power wash and Krylon rebuild, Randy crowned the small-block with a Holley 750 and swap meet manifold, adding R.E.D. headers (with collector baffles) and Accel ignition. Check those motor mounts. The TH350 is stock, as is the 12-bolt rear, but 3.73:1 gears provide a lot of pull. Aluminum Ron Davis radiator with R.E.D. full shroud and Spal fan keep the temp gauge mellow under sadistic Arizona sun. The overflow can is regulation. (Photo Courtesy Randy Ellis Design) *Top Right and Middle:* Military surplus body fluid container (actually a beer cooler) tilts to access fuel and gear lube fill, along with battery, compressor, and solenoids for air bags. Pinion angle appears zoinked here, but goes back to normal with bags inflated. Stereo speakers? I'm guessing these only get used during gas station breaks and picnics. The open headers provide the real soundtrack. (Photos Courtesy Christian Hazel)

Photo shoots can be mind numbingly tedious affairs and Randy is strictly an action figure. Not a good mix. He finally bolted from his pose and was last seen heading northwest at high velocity.

It took me a day and a half to walk back to town.

(Photo Courtesy Vic Macias)

The grille and 9-inch chopped windshield are the only factory Willys body parts ("I didn't have a problem cutting up the windshield frame"). Body shell is fiberglass remains of retired rock crawler. The 15x8 Pro Comp wheels fit 31x10.5 General Grabbers to make extreme gnarl statement, but ride easy. In fact, with some air in the bags, the Jeep feels like driving your couch around. Really. Hey, is that an alien peeking over the crest of the hill? Made you look! (Photo Courtesy Christian Hazel)

Chapter 6

HIGHTAILING IT INTO THE FUTURE

—FEARLESS EXPLORERS DISCOVER FUTURE BASED ON PAST

Matt Springsteen's '56 Willys Jeep pickup.

TONIGHT, ON NEWSWATCH AT 11:00

The evolution isn't over yet. Rats may have lost some of their shock value to exposure, but the fun isn't done—not by a long shot.

As the supply of vintage tin gets picked over, enterprising rodders are turning to alternative raw material to create fresh takes on the DIY ethic. The latest apex in the creative curve is carrying builders to uncharted territory at warp speed, as they consider new ways to skin these old cats. Some are building with "found" materials, while others blueprint construction from carefully considered later-model OEM sources. Some mad ratters are even using 3-D computer software to sketch their next project.

We had a few examples lined up that didn't make our deadline, including a severely narrowed, chopped, and sectioned '70 Ford pickup, a few Volksrods, what appeared to be an early 1930s roadster built entirely from wrecking yard sheet metal (actually well proportioned), more than one Rothesque monster car fabbed from a free-for-all mix of 1970s-vintage body panels, and even an "art car" featuring a body made exclusively from non-automotive materials. Imagination is the only limitation here.

Will flathead-powered hovercraft be passing us, down the road? Whatever happens, sleep well tonight knowing that affordable fun will continue to define the core of the high velocity vortex known as hot rodding. May it continue to flourish, well into future millennia. And here's hoping these samples inspire you to a broader vision of what can be. Imagine it, build it, and drive it.

Pat McNeal's '42 Chevy cabover.
(Photos Courtesy Joe Wongananda)

Pat McNeal
Towing Company Owner
Baltimore, Maryland
1942 Chevy Cabover

The first decibels are alarming as hell. The gasoline-fueled voices of 702 (cubic inches) baritones crescendo on your eardrums with the pressure and intensity of a World War II air strike. As it comes into view, the effect is at once revelatory, shocking, and hilarious. The warning growl and bark that filled the entire atmosphere has emanated from this tiny package, hardly big enough to hold a whispered whimper from an asthmatic chihuahua.

Pat kicked his rat squarely into the future with minimal use of vintage tin and maximum design and fabrication skills. In his many years of running a towing business, you know this guy has seen it all and obviously, some major weirdness got stuck in his head. Pat needed an outlet for the pressure those demonic visions created inside of him.

Yes, it's very much a driver and Pat has longhauled it up and down the East Coast, matching nerve and wits with the big rigs. "This car is no trailer queen. I drove it from Baltimore to Daytona Beach for the Turkey Run, 900 miles each way. She got 12½ mpg at an average speed of 80 mph." It gets regular workouts around town, too. (Photo Courtesy Joe Wongananda)

Photog Joe Wongananda shot Pat's cabover at sundown in this Baltimore industrial complex and just walked away. Cold, huh? Manhole covers and imminent roadkill are usually the only ones to get this view, but no matter how tall you are, the little truck makes a big impression. This angle offers peek at Super Bell axle, hung on Posies spring and steered with a "half rack." (Photo Courtesy Joe Wongananda)

Pat obviously has a keen eye for **proportion,** teamed with strong **metalworking and fabrication** skills.

But some design cues are born of necessity, like those nostrils on the nose. "The hood holes were the result of an overheating problem. I was on my maiden voyage, heading to Latimore Valley for the Jalopyrama. It's amazing what can be accomplished on the side of the road with a hole saw, cordless drill, and a steady hand." But the front-mounted radiator is catching some sick air now. (Photo Courtesy Joe Wongananda)

Top Left and Right: Of course, the big news is kept around back, as a surprise for gawkers making their way around the truck. Semi-popular with the industrial set, the 1961 GMC V-12 (sometimes called a twin six, but sharing a common block, crank, and distributor drive) boasts 702 ci of raw grunt. The W-head imagery makes a dramatic visual, but the reality is even more fun than that. These engines make enough low-end twist (585 ft-lbs, stock) to punt manhole covers 50 yards with the rear tires, just coming off idle. A worked-over Eldorado transaxle sends the kick to a Winters quick-change rear. Check Pat's ladder bars, made from 1940 Ford 'bones. All fab work is top-notch. This guy's good. (Photos Courtesy Joe Wongananda) *Middle Right:* It's roomier than you'd expect inside, thanks to cabover design's flat floor, allowing for low seating. The quick-release aluminum wheel helps, too. Yeah, the 4-inch chopped windshield still cranks out. Stewart-Warner gauges fit right into original dash opening. I dig the big-rig vibe of the shifter handle. Note the Speedway sprint car throttle pedal and Wilwood brake pedal. The SteerClear offset-chain-driven steering coupler (in aluminum housing) got Pat out of a jam the easy way (I love those things). (Photo Courtesy Joe Wongananda) *Bottom:* It cuts an impressive profile, alright. Remember, the top of that cab is chest-high, at best. This angle also shows off the raked nose, 1946 Ford front 'bones, beautifully designed rails, and even the exposed trans case looks organic to the overall design. 4x15 front and 8x17 rear steelies (painted by Inferno Designs) wear 6.40-15 and 8.20-17 Firestones to carry the cartoonie proportions full circle. (Photo Courtesy Joe Wongananda)

Nothing else in Baltimore sounds like *Pat's truck* going through the gears while the quick-change sings harmony!

As the last shards of light shiver away, Pat and son Presley Cash McNeal suit up for the thrill ride home (younger son Pierce couldn't make the photo shoot). The monster fired instantly and they bellowed off into the icy darkness of Baltimore. They do that a lot. A major snowstorm rolled into town that night and settled in for a long stay. (Photos Courtesy Joe Wongananda)

CHAPTER 6: HIGHTAILING IT INTO THE FUTURE   149

Matt Springsteen
Barge Master
Coos Bay, Oregon
1956 Willys Jeep Pickup

Coos Bay is one of those rain-soaked hamlets where the forest meets the ocean in southern Oregon. Seemingly idyllic, yet a decidedly edgy undercurrent lurks about. Turns out, it's a nice place to infect your family with the tetanus bug. That's what Mark Springsteen did and nobody's complaining. Wife Debi, son Matt, and daughter Amy were all exposed from day one and are doing just fine, thank you. Even the dogs, Chief and Coco, get the car thing. Matt got a particularly nasty case, though. A typical Northwest childhood of hot rods, dirt bikes, and 4x4s culminated in driving log trucks with Mark in the family business (although Matt now shuffles oil drums around on ships). Father and son had always spent their off-hours rodding together, so when Matt decided he was ready to build his first rod from scratch, the rite of passage was celebrated with plenty of sparks in the shop.

Matt didn't build a Jeep to make an alternative sheet-metal statement—he and Mark just happened to have a bunch of them laying around—this is definitely Jeep country. And this pickup was epically crusty after sitting in a field for 30 years, so what better to learn on, right? Nobody, including Matt, knew what wonderfully demented vision was lurking in his head. Matt just started hacking and banging (Mark supervised) and a year later, declared the Jeep done. He crawled in for a test drive and hasn't stopped yet.

I dropped in for a weekend with the Springsteens and was chauffeured around the area in the Jeep until lockjaw set in from grinning. It's actually pretty comfy to ride in and you can even see out of it! It fires instantly, goes straight and true, and stops on a dime. Fortunately, none of those dimes were in anyone's pocket. In fact, no one went to jail or even got a ticket (although I was questioned by a Coos County Sheriff at one point). No animals or pedestrians were harmed during our photo shoot either, so I consider it a total success.

The Springsteens are a tight family and gave me a case of the warm fuzzies, welcoming me in, and showing me around the town where everyone knows everyone by name. Of course, everybody in Coos Bay packs a chainsaw, which tends to keep folks pretty polite.

"My favorite part of this is **there are no rules!** That, and building it with **my dad . . .**"

Matt really nailed the proportions, highlighting the elements that make Jeeps so fun. The V'd grille is echoed by a matching front crossmember. The homemade headers help the 351 Ford fill the gap from grille to firewall with interest, so you don't even miss the iconic flat-top fenders. An 8-inch chop is hairy, but the 4-inch channel brings the floor up to your butt, lining up your eyeballs with the teensy windshield. The bed was shortened 3 feet. It's still a Jeep at a glance, but suicide front end, scraping stance (via air bags), and tall rubber evoke an Altered drag car image, mixed with traditional rod details. Great combo!

Taking five, in front of the shop he shares with his dad. This is where the Jeep was built, the latest in a long string of hot rods, 4x4s, dirt bikes, and log trucks that have passed through these doors. Hiding inside on this day were projects from Jeeps to Model As to a Pro/Street Camaro. As Mark says, "We don't specialize in anything!"

Now that Matt's a Barge Master, he has access to floating backdrops. The tugboats pull the barges. This shot shows off the cowbell mounted to the drilled axle. It hits anything taller than 3/4 inch, sounding the warning signal of a charging Brahma bull. Hilarious or annoying, your call (I dig it). Red plexiglass rear window drenches the interior in red light for exotic bordello ambiance.

Left: The 351 Windsor came from Grandpa's cube van that once hauled magazines, then motocross gear. It's mostly stock, but for the Edelbrock 4-barrel and homespun headers. Matt made collectors from 5-inch stainless log truck stacks, split and re-welded for taper. The C-6 transmission from the same van keeps power where it's needed. The A/C compressor ("No idea what it's from") provides air for bags and siren, and the horns are from Matt's old log truck. *Middle:* Mostly original Willys tin in here (steering wheel and column, too), but Matt did some redecorating. He made the stainless seats from log truck rear fenders, the pedals are motorcycle sprockets, and the shifter is from his first big rig. The Faria tachometer still sports Goodwill price tag: $5.00. And Matt taught himself to pinstripe in here. *Right:* The bottomless bed exposes the four-link and spiderweb driveshaft hoop. That fuel tank was previously a big-rig air tank. Left rough cut, the brackets throughout car are fun and functional. Gas can was donated by Grandpa, "just in case." The little Shell emblem at the upper left is a license plate topper, also from Gramps' collection.

The Jeep rolls steady with a dropped early-Ford axle (a wrecking yard find), capped with drilled 1940 Ford brakes. It sports Jeep/Springsteen steering and 9-inch Ford rear with 3.50:1 gears, supported by a homemade triangulated four-link and a home-brew air bag system. All of this sits on the original Jeep rails. We tortured residents and tourists with rowdy exhaust, clanging cowbell, and rattling sheet metal, which inspired rolled-up car windows, some sneers, and lots of smiles.

Don Fields
Semi-retired Carpenter
Grants Pass, Oregon
The Dog

Don's son-in-law Bill seemed to be having all the fun, blasting around from one motorhead gathering to another. Bill's tales of high-speed hijinx finally pushed Don to the breaking point one miserable winter night. Don had been enduring a painfully lengthy layoff from work and was dead broke, cold, tired, and hungry—something had to give. That's the night *The Dog* was born.

Taking inventory of his rural property strewn with decaying motorcycle and automotive carcasses, Don realized he had the makings of something—he just didn't know what it would be until it was finished. Working on pure inspiration and intuition, Don spent the winter head-scratching and tinkering. When the spring thaw came, the shop door rolled up, and this is what rolled out.

Basically built around a Honda V45 Magna sport bike, *The Dog* features a more-eclectic-than-most component mix—Volkswagen front suspension, Model A hood sides, 1947 Chevy hood, turned tail fairing, etc. Don limited himself to parts found on his property to justify the build to baffled wife Joyce.

When the roads dried up, he drove it to town and putted into the local hot spot, stealing the show from some pretty cool hot rods. This is where I met Don, at the Sonic Drive-In. As we spoke, a tremendous rainstorm moved in and the rods scattered like—ironically—rats. Except for *The Dog*. The downpour had me cowering inside my car, with the wipers set on hyperspeed. Squinting through the windshield, I witnessed Don zinging away in *The Dog*, scooping water from his seat and creating the weirdest rooster tail I ever saw.

Don says, "The water sheds pretty good at speed" and the 750-cc quad-carbed Honda got him home quickly, possibly saving him from drowning! But *The Dog*'s maiden voyage passed Don's litmus test and now it's being refined for the open road. "I'd like to take it to the coast [80-some miles] next summer." Are "Dogs" allowed on the beach? I can picture this one chasing tourists across the sand, barking its head off, and wagging its tail. Better bring some poop bags, just in case.

"I was really a pretty **normal guy,** before I came up with this **thing.**"

Okay, let's answer your first question first: Lurking under The Dog's tail is a 750 Honda V45 Magna drivetrain, still mounted to the original Honda frame. These were mid-10-second bikes, stock. This test mule engine is tired, especially the heads. "These heads are such a pain in the ass to work on, I'm swapping in a whole other engine," explains Don. It's water cooled (radiators mount behind the side scoops), uses four carbs ("Plenty of power!"), and the transmission offers enough gear choices to savor the torque curve anywhere, as long as he's going forward. "It doesn't have reverse, so I'm working on an electric wheelchair-type motor to turn the rear wheel backward." The "Gerry Can" is a temporary fuel tank until Don fabs a permanent solution. "Worn out" Harley mufflers provide The Dog a decidedly menacing bark.

Don sacrificed his firewood dolly to make the grille. Hey kids, can you guess what car the "DOG" letters are from? Headlights are actually "old driving lights from somewhere" (made in Chicago). Front suspension, windshield, and hood center strip are early Volkswagen. The hood sides are Model A. The front shocks are Yamaha TT500. The fenders are cut-down Model A spare tire covers. The hood ornament is all that remains of a wrecked Mack log truck. The tailpiece is made from 1947 Chevy Fleetmaster hood. An old "Reno or Bust!" sign that Don got tired of tripping over was volunteered to fill gaps, fab floors, and make rocker panels.

Left and Top Right: Rear view evokes Bert Munro Bonneville imagery, just a bit edgier. The air scoop was made from Suzuki gas tank. The rear ornament evokes early-1930s Pontiac motometer, but actually came off an Avon bottle. Rear lighting appears to be sourced from hardware store. The plate is legit—The Dog is licensed and goes everywhere with Don, on a short leash. *Bottom Right:* Every acreage needs a dead TV sitting in a field to provide the proper atmosphere for creative expression.

Left: Open-air touring is enjoyed in comfort of swap meet poly race seats (note Don's swanky leopard-skin seat cover. Ooh la la!). "Century" badge on swap meet wheel is from old electric fan. The VW speedometer teams with Honda 650 tachometer and idiot light cluster as info center. Don used VW pedals, too. Storage is provided by Army ammo box. A Hurst Indy Shifter (with Honda 125-cc piston knob) selects the gears using patented "Hunt and Find" technology. *Right:* This is where it happened. The Dog was created right here, over a long, cold, wet winter. The season that brings a person face-to-face with his limits, but Don came out feeling groovy thanks to man's best friend! The chopped Honda in background is Don's daily driver.

Don walks The Dog *across his acreage and into the future, wishing us all peace and love. He also mentioned something about kissing his crusty ass goodbye. Although* The Dog *is barely waist-high, Don snuggles down low into it, ensuring perfect hair upon arrival at any destination!*

Some of Don's leftover raw material. He digs Hondas. There's enough here to create a good-size litter of Dog *pups.*

CHAPTER 6: HIGHTAILING IT INTO THE FUTURE

EPILOGUE

What have we learned here? Nothing we didn't already know. Rats still defy definition. Rats still possess amazingly accurate vision, while feigning blindness regarding rulebooks or labels—they're simultaneously throwbacks and visionaries. Rats are still the punch lines to the reality slap of modern life. Rats don't shock as much as educate us—vital as ever, they broadcast their mission statement at full volume to those with fingers in their ears and eyes shut tight against the noise: "Don't take yourself too seriously." I think that's all they're trying to say.

Most importantly, rats are still people, too. I know I'm better off for having met the ones in this book. These people and their cars have been my mirrors, forcing me to look twice at my motives. Perhaps we've been laughing too loudly at their antics to hear the rats discretely telling us that our flies are open. That's what true friends do, while others would only snicker. Rats are our friends.

Like any project, packaging often dictates decisions. That happened with our photo choices and placement. Some were just too fun to toss, so we've included some of them here, as a special feature. Consider this your director's commentary . . .

Matt and Mark Springsteen just happened to have the keys to this mill (they deliver logs there). We took advantage and snapped this father-son portrait, while they discussed truck acceleration dynamics.

Matt: "That whale of yours couldn't get off the line if it was rear-ended by a meteor."
Mark: "No problem. I know yours can't make it 50 feet without something falling off."
Matt: "Oh yeah? I did let you weld some things on it, didn't I?"
Mark: "All part of my plan."
Matt: "You're standing on my foot."
Mark: "Yep."

Uncle Daniel Ferrazin, giving Patricio Germano a metal-working demonstration at San Remo Kustoms. I don't know enough Spanish to translate, but the gist of it was, "Well, that's unfortunate!"

Jerry Fleck and son-in-law Jerid Gunter were constantly tweaking Jerry's Dodge during our photo shoot. They can't help themselves. This roadside throttle linkage adjustment was typical.

Jerry: "Gimme that little screwdriver with the busted top."
Jerid: "You used it for a toothpick, then tossed it out."
Jerry: "Oh yeah. Well, scrape a dime across the road until it'll fit this slot."
Jerid: "I have a nickel and two pennies."
Jerry: (groan) "Scotty, do you have three cents?"

Kristin Martin at Gene Winfield's sheet-metal workshop.

Kristin: "Hey, I'm getting the hang of this lead stuff!"
Gene: "Yeah you are. You just leaded my ring to this door."

Later that day, Kristin donated Studie's battery to Winfield's "The Thing" coupe, when its power cell expired at the El Mirage season opener. Even Steven.

Kristin Martin with her Grease Girls gang, flying their colors in preparation for heavy ground action. Write your own dialog for this shot.

EPILOGUE

After our frigid winter photo shoot, Pat McNeal was ready for the spring thaw! He celebrated at the Jalopy Showdown by giving the truck this macrobiotic facial. The kneejerk reaction was to crank open the windshield for vision's sake, not realizing he was opening the mud gate. Pat kept the hammer down for two laps, as the cab filled to beyond capacity with the guck. And he's still laughing.

CC demonstrates his Morris' "giving birth" driving position. 10-second runs are one thing, but the Morris has done a couple of Americruises and is now hungry for Drag Week and/or Power Tour.

Silas Warren approached Troy Wascher's Pontiac with caution for this shot. Good thing—this turned out to be a dangerous situation. We can't reveal any details until the trial is over.

After an epic maiden-voyage drive to Bonneville Speed Week, Kristin Martin's Studebaker naturally gravitated to hobnob with its crusty cousins. They were definitely a bad influence. Rumor has it, Kristen picked up a rule book at the event.